God Ungod Divine

Reflections on Sebastian Kappen's Writings

God Ungod Divine

Reflections on Sebastian Kappen's Writings

Sebastian Vattamattam

2022

God Ungod Divine: Reflections on Sebastian Kappen's Writings — published by the Indian Society for Promoting Christian Knowledge (ISPCK), Post Box 1585, Kashmere Gate, Delhi-110006.

ISBN: 978-93-90569-50-2

Cover image: C.F. John

Laser typeset by

ISPCK, Post Box 1585, 1654, Madarsa Road, Kashmere Gate, Delhi-110006
• *Tel:* 23866323

e-mail: ashish@ispck.org.in • ella@ispck.org.in
website: www.ispck.org.in

Sebastian Vattamattam, born in 1945, is a nephew of Sebastian Kappen. He is a retired professor of mathematics and a writer. He has taught in S. B. College, Changanassery; Loyola School, Goa; Dutse Teachers College, Nigeria; and Pakshama School, Qatar.

In Malayalam he has authored the books: *Ecology and Culture* (with Fr. Kappen), *Language and Power, Unconscious Travels of Language – From Freud to Lacan, Ideology and Symbolic Revolution, Sigmund Freud, What Dreams Tell Us*, and *Jesus and Marx in Fr. Kappen's Thoughts*.

Vattamattam has compiled, and edited many books of Fr. Kappen, including his collected works.

I, for one, am wary of being called a Christian. I see myself
as a disciple of Jesus, who has been profoundly influenced
by the teachings of the Buddha and, in theology at least,
by the *Siva-Sakti* conception of the divine, going back to
the pre-*aryan* culture."

Sebastian Kappen

Contents

Sebastian Kappen: The Person and His Passion

Mercy Kappen

It is difficult to speak about Kappen without speaking about his politics and his passion, his perspectives, and his practice. Kappen transcended the dichotomies of personal and political, private and public in his life. The pain and frustration, the anger and anxieties he experienced in the dailiness of his life were so much linked to the larger socio-political structures and systems. Be it the Bhopal Gas Genocide, the Gulf war, or the demolition of the Babri Masjid – all these were also his private pain. In fact, his first heart attack happened when he was giving a lecture at the SEARCH institute in Bangalore. He was talking about the injustices and inhumanity of war when he experienced severe chest pain and was rushed to Philomena's Hospital. His personal pains were rooted in and inextricably linked with the historical and political context of his time.

Kappen made personal choices that were consistent with his politics. This is reiterated by his activist-scholar friends. Ramdas, one of his close associates, wrote in a condolence letter to me,

"Kappen must be commemorated. However, it is important, how it is done. .. Personally, I owe him a lot. Most of my clarity on issues and understanding of basic philosophy was acquired at his feet between 1975 and '79. Reflecting upon him dispassionately, I think that it was not so much what he said that was so radically different, but that he dared all his life to go it alone. He sought his security in his commitment rather than his religious trappings. He walked his own path. When one talks of what Kappen said, the spirit of the man must also come through. For that, I believe, is his message. And it is that spirit that must continue to challenge the status quo. We need not be in a hurry because Kappen won't be forgotten soon" (5th January 1994).

Kappen's decision to move out of the comforts and confines of Jesuit houses was part of this conviction that he should be living with people experiencing the uncertainties, insecurities, and vulnerabilities of life in the margins. As Artist C F John says,

> "Kappen knew the rise and fall of prices of essential commodities and its impact on common people, as well as the rise and fall of authoritarian regimes and its impact on the social fabric."

He used to ask his young friends, whether they knew the price of rice, sugar, tea, or vegetables. 'Do you know how long you have to stand in the queue to get a can of kerosene oil?' He would ask. He cooked his own food, on a kerosene stove. Not just his food. He also cooked for the students, artists, activists, and academics that used to gather for study sessions in his single room asbestos roofed house in an urban poor locality in Chennai and later in Bangalore. In fact, I learned my basic cooking from him. Also the basics of Marxism, Liberation Theology, Ecology, Feminism – everything that's required to be a conscious human being.

The first gift I received from Kappen was a bible – Good News for Modern Man. He told me to read at least one page every day. 'It would help to improve your English', he said. Wish I had followed his advice. During vacations, I used to go and stay with Kappen. I helped him with his typing and sat through several study classes. Kappen was a perfectionist not just in his writing but also in his sweeping and cleaning and washing. I used to wonder why he gets so agitated with the printer about a missing comma. It took me several years to realise the huge difference the presence or absence of a comma can make to your meaning. Much later, I also understood the implications of being in a state of coma to the realities around, of not developing a critical consciousness and transformative praxis.

Kappen meticulously prepared for the study sessions he used to conduct. He never took us for granted, instead instilled in us the thirst for knowledge and the courage to question the status quo. He had the capacity to explain the most complicated concepts with the simplest and everyday examples and stories with an unmatched sense of humour. I can still hear his cheerful and thunderous laughter as he narrated the adventures of gods and goddesses, saints, and seers at his sessions on Tradition and Modernity at the United Theological College in Bangalore. These lectures were compiled and edited by him for publication under the title, *Tradition, Modernity, Counterculture – An Asian Perspective.*[1] It was published posthumously by Visthar and has gone into several reprints.

At a Kappen Memorial Lecture, Prof. Babu Mathew, academic and trade unionist, recollected how meticulous Kappen was. 'He never spoke in any superficial manner. He would have pondered several hours over every word he uttered.' There was a man who sat late in the night with a cup of coffee/tea smoking away, sitting and continuously reading, reflecting, making notes before going to take a session or deliver a lecture. As a result of their exposure to Kappen, many activists and students in the 1970s and 80s got involved both in radical theology as well as the left movement. Looking back on his life Babu Mathew acknowledges that 'the single most important influencing factor that made him join the communist movement in India was Fr. Kappen's contribution. We don't know whether Kappen intended that as he was equally critical of both the Church and the Party'.

Moderating a Kappen memorial meeting in Bangalore, Sadanand Menon, academic and arts editor, spoke about how 'being anarchic by temperament he could not acknowledge discipleship or owe allegiance to any set of ideas or thinkers. However, without any qualm, he could accept Kappen as one of his gurus. During the political emergency in the 70s, Menon and friends felt the need to temper activism with deeper reflection, and Kappen was their obvious choice to lead them through the maze of radical political philosophies. This stimulating series of study classes called Socialist Forum lasted for about four years.

Authenticity was one of Kappen's favourite words. He had no patience for hypocrisy and double standards. He assessed people on the basis of the gaps between their precepts and practice. Many even in the close circle of friends found his ways uncompromising. One of the Kappen Memorial lectures we organised was titled "The Beauty of Compromise". That was the title given by the speaker, renowned historian Ramachandra Guha. An activist, who was associated with Kappen, called and questioned us as to how we could have a memorial lecture on 'Beauty of Compromise' for a person who never compromised.

I am fortunate to have been 'mothered' and mentored by Kappen. I have perplexed many, curious about how I am related to Kappen, by saying that he was my mother. By his very being, he challenged the binaries of feminine and masculine, emotional and rational, spiritual and material. He sacrificed buying his favourite titles to support my hostel and college fees. Kappen was concerned whether I was fluttering through life without anchoring myself in any one discipline or field of involvement. Those were the initial years of Visthar. I used to go to him with the concept notes and introductions I wrote. He was not happy that I was moving from one seminar to the other. On one occasion when I went to correct a circular I wrote on the New Economic Policy (NEP), Kappen challenged me to engage him in a conversation on the topic, which

I could not. I had just read enough to draft that letter inviting participants. I was disappointed and upset that I could not take on his challenge. But today I am so grateful for the challenge he posed me to focus and deepen, to be rooted before branching.

Kappen detested intellectual hollowness and dishonesty. This was evident in his response to the censorship of his book Jesus and Freedom by the Congregation for the Doctrine of Faith. Kappen wrote,

> "The book, Jesus and Freedom, is the crystallization of my basic convictions regarding Jesus and his message. So much so, for me to deny its central message would amount to sheer intellectual dishonesty and a betrayal of my mission as a disciple of Jesus."[2]

Kappen considered himself a disciple of Jesus and not a disciple of the Church. He believed that

> "Jesus could not come to his own within the official Christianity. Dogma reified him; theology reduced him to a sum of concepts: cult degraded him to a god among the many gods. His visage was further marred and mutilated by Christianity's alliance with the rulers and the principalities of this world."[3]

As we know, Kappen's theological stances evoked strong criticism in traditional circles of the Church and his book *Jesus and Freedom* was banned from Seminaries. Kappen responded to the censorship of his book with a pamphlet entitled "Censorship and the Future of Asian Theology." The response reflected his bold and un-compromising stand. He experienced tremendous stress during those days as if he feared that he would be expelled from the Society of Jesus, the membership of which he valued most. I think the post-nominal letters 'S J' had a much deeper, spiritual and political meaning for him, beyond what it was meant to be. He used to say that it is not he who should be out but those who censored his writings, who owed their allegiance to the establishment and not to Jesus, the prophet.

The Transition from a Pietistic Priest to a Prophet

In his autobiographical notes, Kappen writes about his early years in the Society of Jesus, how so deeply ingrained in him those days was the belief that the priest held the key to heaven. How he was all consumed by the zeal to become a saint and how he did prayers with a vengeance. He strove to be the first to enter the chapel and the last to quit. Years later he would give up once and for all the ambition of becoming a saint. 'With that I regained peace' he writes.

It is from a liberative perspective that Kappen makes a strong critique of the Church. He writes,

> "The fear of sin coupled with frustrated sexuality is at the root of the oppressiveness that is found in the Churches - aggressiveness that takes the form of over discipline, regimentation, authoritarianism, and dogmatism. The sense of sin also underpins the political economy of the Church. Take away the fear of sin, there will be fewer people at Sunday Masses, fewer people to make confessions, fewer to receive the sacraments, fewer still to make votive offerings. Churches will remain mostly unfrequented and priests un/under-employed. The end result will be the collapse of ecclesiastical institutions."[4]

Looking at the happenings within the Church today, we realise how prophetic Kappen was in denouncing churchist theology and practice. He advocated a theology that moves toward liberation and justice for all people inclusive of all their differences. A theology that leaves no one's oppression unchallenged and no system of oppression intact. His was a call to build prophetic communities - communities of resistance and hope.

Kappen's Quest for a Counterculture

One of the main concerns of Kappen was the cultural challenges facing the people of India. He saw the process of social transformation as a transition "from inherited cultural bondages to freedom for fashioning a new, humane and humanizing culture." He believed that a new social order could be brought about only by those individuals and groups who play the role of prophets, who protest against oppressive systems, who dare to dissent and usher in a counterculture. "For dissenting behaviour is precisely what signals and provokes change. What is revolution but organized dissent?" Kappen wrote in Negations, a journal of culture and creative praxis he edited.[5]

In the essay titled "Towards an Alternative Cultural Paradigm," Kappen dwells in detail on the cultural prerequisites for an alternative model of development. He wrote,

> "Culture must body forth not only into the political organization of society and into specifically culture pursuits, but also into homogenizing cultural imperialism. Every aspect of our economic life must bear the signature of our culture. The right to alterity and cultural identity must be affirmed as a fundamental human right. Hence the historic challenge to fight the homogenizing cultural imperialism."[6]

The Final Journey

In the second half of 1993, Kappen began writing his autobiographical notes. He wrote how intimately his being, spirit, and flesh, was bound up with the earth of his village. Out of the 15 pages he wrote, two were about his parents. "Of all those who peopled my past, my father is the most present."

> "If ever there was a man to whom work was play and passion rolled into one, that was my father. Invariably I accompanied him to the field tilled and ploughed and planted with him until, on warm days, salt formed on my back, something that did me and my father proud. By noon I would be exhausted, covered with mud, and bathed in sweat. For me, those were moments of intense contentment, when I experienced the drunkenness of being and being well?"[7]

He continues,

> "There is much I learned from my father – the humanizing and ludic character of work, the therapeutic effects of communion with nature, the conviction that much of what goes by religion is sham and hypocritical. More importantly, he instilled in me the mystique of striving. In 1944 as I was getting into the bullock cart

that was to drive me away from home for good, and my relatives and neighbours had gathered to say good-bye, my father had only this to say, 'Wherever you go, try to excel.' That advice I have conscientiously followed whether in the pursuit of spirituality, the study of humanities or mastery of philosophies. ... In the Society of Jesus too I excelled but that was as a dissenter."[8]

During 1993, Kappen had the nostalgic longing to visit his place of birth, the house he was born in, the land where he used to work with his father before joining the Society of Jesus. I was to accompany him. We had booked our tickets to go to Kerala on 21st December. He was very excited about the visit and we did meticulous planning. That trip was destined not to happen. Kappen returned to the earth on November 30th, 1993, three weeks before we were to travel to Kodikulam, his native village.

Reflecting on death, he had written in his diary,

"On dying, I shall re-join the Divine, the telluric divine, the divine whose home is the earth, the visible universe. I shall not leave the earth but return to it."

I conclude with a few lines from "When Great Trees Fall" by my favourite poet Maya Angelou:

"...Great souls die and our reality,
Bound to them, takes leave of us.
Our souls, dependent upon their nurture, now shrink.
Our minds formed and informed by their radiance, fall away.
We are not so much maddened
as reduced to the unutterable ignorance of dark, cold caves.
And when great souls die,
after a period peace blooms, ...
Spaces fill with a kind of soothing electric vibration.
Our senses, restored, never to be the same, whisper to us.
They existed. They existed.

We can be. Be and be better.

For they existed."

(Paper presented at the National Seminar in honour of Sebastian Kappen S J, 11-12 October 2019 at Ernakulum, Kerala)

Notes

1. Collected Works of Sebastian Kappen, ISPCK, Delhi, Vol.6, Part 1.
2. Vol.1, p.327.
3. Vol.3, p.75.
4. Vol.6, p.219-20.
5. Vol.2, p.226.
6. Vol.6, p.120.
7. Vol.6, p.215.
8. Vol.6, p.218.

Thinking of Him is a Joy

C. F. John

The last conversation I had with Fr. Sebastian Kappen was in the evening of 28 November 1993, two days before he returned to Mother Earth. The conversation was around one of his paintings. It had a pond in the center, with a crane on its bank, and was surrounded by flowering trees, creepers, and grass. The painting presented calmness, peace, joy and celebrated the diversity of life. My question was about the presence of the crane. "It stays calm and meditative. But on second thought we would realise that it is waiting to devour a fish from the pond. Isn't that something unsettling?!" I asked him. He said, "The crane must be thinking that the fish in the pond can attain mukti only if she devours it," and he laughed. I joined him too. The next day my father returned to his True Home and the day after that Kappen too.

I feel this last line I heard from him has something to speak of his concerns with the dogmas of our times. He cared not to indulge in speculative thinking but to make direct contact with the Being, and to understand the unfolding of mysteries Life. He understood the need to be cautious of the light in which one sees and interprets the world, which compelled him to be part of the prophetic tradition. The cause of much of our sorrow and tension comes from our interpretations. Though at one level the revealing of the world from time to time brings forth beauty, mystery, and wonder, at another, when it is propelled by the self-interest of the individual, family, class, community, religion, or nation affecting not only others but also the Earth and Life itself, it becomes a matter of concern.

I was very fortunate to have had the opportunity to closely connect with S. Kappen during the last six years of his life. My acquaintance with him helped deeply to reassure me of my own perspectives with regards to Earth and Life, which includes an Earth-centered spirituality, culture, social equity, and politics. Particularly to see these thoughts, not merely as perspectives but more importantly a way of living. The opportunity to witness his life was a gift because what I seek mostly are not ideas and perspectives but embodied visions. Kappen was one. He continues to give conviction, strength, and courage.

Fr. S. Kappen

I heard of the then controversial name, S. Kappen, among Christian circles many years before I got the opportunity to meet him. It happened in 1987. He had agreed to write and present a paper on art and social consciousness in a seminar that I had organised under the banner of Pipal Tree, Bangalore, on the theme of "Struggles for Social Change and Art". It was the beginning of my reading of Kappen and of spending time with him. He moved to Bangalore in 1988 from Thiruvananthapuram and since then till the end, I spent time with him most evenings.

He as a person and his thoughts started growing in me in a manner that had the deepest bearing on me. I have not read much of his writings concerning theology, though he is known largely for such writings, but his later writings. Most of them are published posthumously in the book *Tradition Modernity Counterculture* by Visthar and those readings have served for me as a vital reference to this day. I have read it again and again, and each time it opens up fresh and alive.

Meticulous Kappen

Anyone closely connected to Kappen would know how meticulous he was in his care for the details when it came to writing, and how uncompromising he was with regards to spelling and other details when it came to publishing a book.

Yes, he was very meticulous in the use of words, the arrangement of words to make sentences, and the arrangement of sentences to make paragraphs. No extra words would be used. Each word was weighed and then placed. He did not feel content with using words from his known vocabulary but instead would look for appropriate words to express what he wanted to express. Even if it meant introducing us to a new word, he would take courage to do so.

When he is needed to give a talk in Malayalam, he would start preparing himself a week in advance—not his thoughts but his tongue. He would read out loud, record his reading and listen for the clarity of its sounds, accents, and flow.

His Writing

However difficult the subject may be, he wrote in such a way that any person could understand it, provided he or she was willing to sit and read with the intent to understand. He broke down the thoughts into sections and illustrated the ideas with examples. He did not present any thought as an abstraction, with either the hope of giving or the fear of losing its 'halo' of profundity. But rather he revealed the subject matter's profundity by taking us to its elemental beauty.

His presentations were like taking a bundle of tangled threads, untying each knot by pulling out each thread and spreading them for us to investigate and weave back into a beautiful new whole.

To understand an article written by Kappen, we need not have read a number of other books, articles, or isms. He took the effort to make the thoughts complete in themselves. This does not mean that Kappen did not root his thought in isms, philosophical schools, and other thinkers. But the difference is that Kappen had a way of unwrapping his articulation in such a way so that the reader could follow him.

Simple Living

He lived a simple life. He spent his last three years in a small rented space of about 200 square feet on the first floor of a house in Sevanagar. The house contained only essential items, minimal to the core. Periodically he disposed of even the books that were not essential to him anymore. His entire collection of books fitted in a small open rack. Till the end, he cooked on a kerosene stove. His food was very simple. He would put rice and vegetables all together and boil and eat. He not only knew the rise and fall of the prices of vegetables and all other essential food items and their impact on common people but also the rise and fall of world powers and its impact on the social fabric. To name a few events that happened during the last few years of his life: the pulling down of the Berlin Wall, the collapse of the USSR, the signing of New Economic Policy, the War on the Gulf by the US Bush government, the demolition of Babri Masjid and the emergence of religious fundamentalism in India. He had only two sets of clothes and a jacket which he washed himself. The only indulgence we saw him committing occasionally was buying an apple cake for Rs. 5. That too he would share with us. He was fond of caramel custard too, which he treated us with on a couple of occasions.

He used to write his articles by hand, carrying out all corrections using correcting fluid, and only at the end did the typing using his small and old portable typewriter. Pressing any of its buttons was hard. After his bypass surgery, it was particularly straining for him to type on it. He once expressed the desire that if he had an electronic typewriter to reduce the stress from typing.

When Kappen made a correction to a word in his handwritten article, he would retain whatever spelling from the existing word he could into the new. For example, if the word CORRECTION needed to be changed to CORRESPOND, he would retain the first five letters, CORRE, strikeout CTI, write SP over it, retain ON and add the D. That made it read CORRESPOND. It is not just about making the necessary spelling corrections in a word, but also about everything else we meet with in life, in thinking, in acceptance, and embracing. He applied such detailed attention to everything he did. When we remain within limits, it heightens our perspective on what minimum to be removed and all that is to be retained. Today we are abundant with tools and machines, which enable us to eliminate and replace mindlessly. Like removing all that were there in a large terrain of land and leveling it with an earth mover to replant the new.

His monthly budget, needless to say, was minimal. Hence anything bought was only after much consideration. If he wanted to buy a book, he would make sure if the book was essential for him. His regular place for the books was Premier Bookstore, a tiny shop stocked with books up to the ceiling, a favourite place for all thinkers, writers, and serious book lovers. People like Ramchandra Guha, U. R. Ananthamurthy, Girish Karnad, and anyone else you could name all frequented this place. He would visit the book store, browse through a book that he found relevant to his thinking, note the price, and return it to the shelf. After some days he would visit again to see if he should buy it. After several days he would go again, only then, if needed he would buy the book. The light of his writing takes its bearing from this minimal, mindful and conscious living.

It is said that if a shoe is made perfectly, we do not become conscious of it when we wear it. So were Kappen's presentations. When he spoke he sculpted his words so that we heard him right, both in sound and silence, without being conscious of the accent. When we read his writings it is like a world being revealed and simultaneously a mystery waiting to be opened. According to the willingness of the reader, the text reveals itself. We engage with it as a play of hide and seek rather than being conscious of the words that he used. This is true of all that Kappen was and is. When I think of Kappen as a person, an image that comes to my mind is of a rock, wet with springs of sweet water flowing from it, and tender plants growing around it and giving it a canopy.

His Paintings

Kappen did a total of 17 artworks. One of which was a collage and another a drawing. Four paintings are on a canvas board of 21"×14" in size, one is on a 30"×30" canvas, and 10 are on oil sketching paper of about 8"×11" in size.

Roughly four of them are an attempt to affirm and reclaim the sensuous world that I think he felt was suppressed during his priestly formation. One is of a young lady with her baby sitting under a tree on a riverside. Another one is of a young girl trying to sense the fragrance of a flower from a plant on the bank of a river. Both are vibrant in colours. The collage is about questions of existence, entering the unknown and mysterious world through death, renouncing the name and form.

Two paintings absorb me consistently, along with a few other supporting smaller works. One is of a family sitting together in a rock cave in the presence of an oil lamp. A grandmother, a couple, and their son, like an icon of a family. Both the ladies look inward, the man to the distance and the child straight to the viewer demanding attention. This work expresses great interiorization. The presence of light gives a sense of assurance.

The other is of a lady walking up to a stream flowing down between two rocks. She is old and weak, dangling a cloth bag from one hand and with the other hand holding a walking stick. Ignoring her age and physical condition, she strives on her way, reaching the grace of life that is gushing down like a waterfall. Though one senses a bit of tension considering her age and weakness, the painting absorbs and soaks us with peace, with the bold assertion of a transcending reality, presented in the form of two rocks covering much of the canvas and the stream gushing down between them, which one aspires to enter. It also holds the suggestion of the vast blue sky, the springing forth of green life, and strokes of yellow sharing warmth. It is simultaneously firm in the rocks, dynamic in the flowing water, and fragile and vulnerable, in the seeker.

The other supporting works also express a sense of surrendering to a reality that shares a time beyond this time. The presence of water is an important element in all of these works —water as a symbol for nurturing, healing, and transcending. They have something primordial in them, of a seeker living in the presence of what she or he is seeking.

Mindful Living

We hear of conscious breathing, mindful living, and being in the present. Our being in the present would gain a realm of prophetic vision if we are mindful about the moment which also has a historical and cultural and social bearing.

Kappen sought the Being of beings that make a play between concealing and revealing—as between word and meaning, world and earth, and Parvathy and Parameshwara in the opening of Kalidasa's Raghuvamsa. It is about the unfolding of the mystery of creation and the creation of worlds within the world. It links deeply with his affirmation and reclaiming of Eros for the full blossoming of all. He writes,

> "As an essential dimension of human existence, Eros must shape all cultures. But it can fully realise itself only when it is controlled by love understood as concern for the well-being of oneself and the

community. Such control is basic repression and no social order can do without it. What thwarts Eros and impoverishes societal life is what Herbert Marcuse calls 'surplus repression', that is, the repression of the Eros of the many for the benefit of the privileged few. Whether that benefit be in terms of pleasure or power."[1]

His writings are prophetic, simultaneously spiritual and visionary. He wrestles with theories and perceptions of our times that thwart the blossoming of all. His wrestling with dogmas, though widely interpreted from the point of view of social justice, is deeply founded on a spiritual vision, rooted in earth and life, celebrating a biotic-spiritual continuum. This comes out beautifully when he writes about art. His writing on art is not about art alone but of our whole existence. He writes:

"Art opens up and exhibits a dimension of reality that is not accessible either to common observation or to scientific investigations... The being of any reality is how it concretely appears to us with all the wealth of its meanings. Take, for instance, the pen in my hand. It is not just something to write with. Through the material of which it is made, it is linked to the earth, the common home and mother of humans and things. The pen is also the visible bond that binds me to the reading and writing community. It points to the place I occupy in society . . . as a tool that was invented at a particular stage in history and destined to go out of use in course of time. It is also bound up with the story of human inventiveness and human destiny as a whole. Seen from this angle it is not just an object standing out there in opposition to me, the subject. On a deeper level it is in me and I in it."[2]

Let me close this reflection by offering you one more quote from Kappen. A transcending vision and trust that hold us together beyond identity politics.

"The recognition of the earth as our common mother provides a new basis for the kinship of humans with one another and with nature. All living creatures, human as well as nonhuman, spring up from the earth and, in the end, return to it. Religions may war against religions: gods may overthrow gods: and nations, other nations. But the earth will ever remain undivided against herself. For, all earth is one Earth. As such She binds together the many and the diverse. Each different grouping maintaining its own customs and speech."[3]

(Article published in the Malayalam Journal, Ezhuthu Masika, 2019 December)

Notes

1. Vol.6, p.64.

2. Vol.6, p.99.

3. Vol.6, p.62.

Introduction
The Destiny and Plight of Prophets
Josy Joseph

Towards the end of this book, the author quotes the famous biblical statement: "A prophet will always be held in honour except in his hometown, and among his kinsmen and family" (Mark 6:4). These words apply to the subject of this monograph – Sebastian Kappen.

Kappen was a brilliant and original thinker who had that rare and felicitous blend of creative and critical intelligence. He radicalised Theology, infusing it with the rigours of critical theory, social commitment as well as ethical responsibility.

Whenever I think of Kappen, I am reminded of Osho Rajneesh's brilliant joke about Karl Marx going to heaven. Here's a rough paraphrase: Every month, St. Peter and Lucifer meet to divide the newly arrived souls between them. When Karl Marx turned up, Lucifer had to take the atheist to hell. After a month, Peter sees Lucifer in a horrible condition – one horn is broken, the tail burned and the face all pale. It appears that Marx had organised the inmates of hell and led a revolt against Lucifer. Lucifer pleads with Peter to take Marx to heaven for just a month, so that he can recover from the shock. In the next monthly meeting, Lucifer is surprised to find Peter happy, relaxed, and in praise of Marx.

Peter tells Lucifer that he had several pleasant discussions with his cultured guest. When Lucifer wonders, "Indeed? But what does God say?" Peter replies: "Oh, come on, Lucifer, You know God doesn't exist!"

What has this joke to do with Kappen? Well, here's the analogy: the Jesuit order of the Catholic Church sends Kappen to Europe in the 1950s, so that he will learn Marxism thoroughly and help the Church in countering its arguments. Several years later, Kappen returns, having completed his studies and even writing a doctoral thesis on Marxian Atheism. By now, not only is he a confirmed Marxist but a staunch critic of the ways of the mainstream Church as well.

Kappen goes on to write several significant works that analysed the inter-relation between the individual, society, and the cosmos. His was a mind that was far ahead of the times. A prophetic thinker, he was one of the earliest in this part of the world to talk consistently about such ideas as Liberation Theology, Deep Ecology, Gender equality, and Secular Spirituality. In addition to his deep knowledge of Marxism, Kappen was also well versed in the various schools of Western Philosophy. He did not believe in accumulating knowledge for its own sake. He rather considered knowledge worthless unless it helped in improving the individual and the world around. He was a philosopher who practised critical consciousness and attempted to bring about a transformative praxis.

He was a rare 'public intellectual' in the sense Edward Said uses the term – a critical insider and a disrupter of status quo. He was genuine and authentic (one of his favourite words), who practised what he preached. He never tried to become a guru or get famous. In fact, he was often misunderstood and isolated by the powers that be.

Prof. Sebastian Vattamattam has inherited from Fr. Kappen, his uncle, and mentor, this fierce commitment to truth as well as the relentless and passionate pursuit of knowledge. Like Kappen, he too has often been misunderstood and criticised for challenging the structures of power. The guardians (and beneficiaries) of the status quo have often considered him an enemy. But he has steadfastly carried on his intellectual life, producing work after work of the highest quality and lasting value (having published around 20 titles till date). Prof. Vattamattam is also one of the few Malayalis who have mastered the complex ideas of Jacques Lacan, Slavoj Žižek, and many other profound thinkers.

He was the leader of the team that discovered and brought to light the prodigious talent and knowledge of Mariamma Chedathy, one of Kerala's greatest folklorists. He has also been responsible (often single-handedly) for preserving the work of Kappen for posterity. Prof. Vattamattam has spent a lifetime reading, editing, translating, and eventually publishing the works of Kappen in both English and Malayalam. All of us ought to be grateful to him for this selfless labour of love. And now comes this wonderful little book that captures the essence of his lifelong obsession with Kappen's thought. I cannot imagine a better title for this work. "God, Ungod, and the Divine" are indeed the keywords of Kappen's critical engagement with the concept. If 'God' stands for the popular understanding of the concept, 'Ungod' is Kappen's term for what the institutions and structures of organised religion have made IT to be; while 'the Divine' is Kappen's alternative paradigm. This book is not just a reductive summary of Kappan's ideas, but a reflective response to them. Often, the author elaborates an argument and applies it to the contemporary socio-political context. At times, he gives his own radical interpretations and critical analyses as well.

I consider it an honour to be associated with this wonderful work by my former teacher. And I sincerely hope that every reader will be enlightened and liberated by the 'authentic' thoughts of the illustrious Kappen, beautifully distilled and critically reinterpreted here by his illustrious disciple. In a sense, this is a contemporary instance of the great dialogic tradition of philosophy itself, going all the way back to Socrates and Plato.

Foreword

Josy compares Fr. Kappen to a prophet. What comes to my mind is a letter Kappen wrote to me while he was living in Trivandrum. He wrote, "Hope I can stay here at least for a year. But there are some ominous signs in the sky. Yesterday I came to know that the Latin bishop has written to the provincial objecting to my stay here in TVM and that the provincial is coming to see me. The write-ups in Kalakaumudi[1] and the Illustrated Weekly[2] must have come to the notice of the bishop. In any case, I am not going to budge. Let them do what they like." Yes, Kappen was a prophet 'held in honour except in his hometown, and among his kinsmen and family'.

After Kappen died in 1993, I decided to collect and publish all his writings in English and Malayalam. With the Collected Works, I have completed the English part of the work. While working on it, Shibin Joseph, a research scholar from JNU came to discuss with me the philosophical aspects of Kappen's writings. Subsequently, he organized a few online talks by me for a group of JNU students. The present book has its origin in the notes I prepared for the talks.

In this book, I haven't gone far into Kappen's personal life and visions. That work I have passed over to two more eligible persons, Mercy, and John, both closely related to Kappen.

Being a professor of Mathematics, I am not very confident about my proficiency in English. So, I sought the help of Josy, my former Math student and now an English Professor. He has done the corrections well, I think. Also, he has written a beautiful introduction to the book, of course with some exaggerated comments on me. After all, he is my student.

I hope this book will serve as a general introduction to Kappen's writings.

Let me express my gratitude to Mercy Kappen, and C F John for their contributions and Josy Joseph for his introduction. The cover image of this book is John's artistic creation. Also, I am grateful to ISPCK for taking up the publication of this book.

Sebastian Vattamattam

Endnotes

1. P. Govindappilla, "To Marx through Christ: The Revolution Created by Kappen", Kalakaumudi, 488, January 20, 1985, continued in the next two issues.

2. Sebastian Kappen, "In Search of a New God", the Illustrated Weekly of India, Bombay, June 9-15, 1985; CW, Vol.4, Chap.1

1

Life and Thoughts of Kappen

Sebastian Kappen was a Jesuit theologian, who laid the foundation for an Asian Theology of Liberation. He was born in Kerala in 1924. Having Joined the Jesuit Society in 1944, he did his theology course in Pune. There he learned two new languages, Greek, and Sanskrit. Proficiency in Greek enabled him to read Heidegger, who had great influence on him. In the last period of his life, I found Kappen translating Heidegger's book *Der Urprung Des Kunstwerkes* from German to his mother tongue, Malayalam. I asked him why he was so eager to do that despite his ill health. He replied that it was his obligation to Heidegger. In many of Kappen's writings, we can see the shadow of *Heideggerian philosophy.*

Knowledge of Sanskrit enabled Kappen to read Vedas, Upanishads, and Puranas. He quotes them in many of his writings on Indian cultural traditions, compiled and published as the book, *Hindutva and Indian Religious Traditions.*[1] There is another book of Kappen, *Tradition Modernity Counterculture,*[2] that contains "Vedic Orientations for a Relevant Ecosophy" as the fifth chapter. Here we can see how his Sanskrit knowledge helped Kappen develop his Ecosophical perspectives.

Now, let us come back to Kappen's life. For his doctorate in theology, he was sent to Rome in the 1950s. That time, the Communist Party of India was gaining political strength in Kerala. Kappen's superiors thought of making him an intellectual crusader against Communism and advised him to take Marxism as his research topic. He went to Rome and started reading Marx. Soon he found that many of Marx's early writings like *Grundrisse* were not available then in English. So, first he studied German language and then came to Marx. He came out with his thesis on Marx's "Economic and Philosophical Manuscripts." So, German is the third language that made Kappen a philosopher, specialized in Marxian philosophy. His doctoral thesis is summarized in *Marxian Atheism,*[3] a book going deep into the original Marx, free from later interpretations. Later, in his Journal 'Negations', Kappen wrote a series of articles on Hegelian and Marxian Dialects, and also a strong critique of the Communist Parties in India for not taking the cultural praxis seriously. These are collected in *Marx beyond Marxism.*[4] Throughout Kappen's writings, his approach is remarkably dialectical.

Kappen's Writings

In 1961, Kappen came back to India. For creating anti-Communist awareness among the youth, he was asked to give intellectual leadership to the student organization ICUF. He started doing that, together with another likeminded theologian Samuel Rayan. But in the study classes and workshops, Kappen told the students about the close similarity between Marx's classless society and the kingdom of God, proclaimed by Jesus, and about the need for revolution for the creation of the kingdom. Very soon he could draw a large number of students, intellectuals, and activists to his side.

In 1972, Kappen's first book, *From Faith to Revolution*, in Malayalam, was released. In the book, he evaluates Marxism in the light of the Bible and Christianity in the light of Marxism, and concludes that only through the synthesis of Marxism and the Bible can the forces of human liberation evolve.

Next year, Kappen's second book, that too in Malayalam, came out: *A Sexual Morality for Tomorrow*. This book exposed the hypocrisy of Malayalees in sexual matters. He affirmed that sex without love was a crime, and that sexual violence was more prevalent among married people. Also, he questioned the negative approach of the Christian and the Indian religious traditions to *Kama*. Later on, in his essay, 'Vedic Orientations' mentioned above, Kappen returns to the question of *Kama*, making it central to his Ecosophy. He wrote a poem, his only poem, 'What the Thunder Says'[5] which begins with the lines,

"In the beginning was Man,

And Man was Desire (*Kama*)."

In 1973, Kappen started living independently of the Jesuit Society. He lived in rented houses, in the ordinary dress just as an ordinary man. For a certain period, he lived in a labour colony in an industrial area in Kochi, together with another Jesuit, Jose Vattamattam, my brother, giving orientation classes to the labourers. He lived in Calicut, Delhi, Chennai, Bangalore, and Trivandrum; again in Bangalore, where he returned to Mother Earth on 30 November 1993. Mother Earth is the centre of Kappen's ecosophical thoughts.

Kappen went on writing and lecturing extensively on the cultural restructuring of Indian society. In 1977, he founded 'Centre for Social Reconstruction' with its office in his house in Madras. Its main activity was organizing study classes on

Marxism, led by Kappen himself. Many such classes were conducted all over India, especially in Kerala. As a result, a team of radical priests, nuns, and youth was formed and it is that team that took initiative in organizing the fish workers' struggle in Kerala in the 1980s.[6]

In the same year, Kappen started publishing two series of booklets called 'Anawim' and 'Socialist Perspectives'; the first introducing Jesus, the prophet from Nazareth, and the second his ideas of socialist revolution. In 1982 he started his 'Negations, a journal of culture and creative praxis.' Though only 13 issues were published, they were all of high standards with contributions from eminent radical thinkers from India and abroad.

In the same year 1977, Orbis Books, New York, published Kappen's first book in English, *Jesus and Freedom*.[7] In this book, he liberates the man Jesus of Nazareth from the Christ of Christianity. This book provoked the Church hierarchy and it was censored by the Vatican. Kappen responded by sending a long reply repudiating the very notion of censorship in the Church, and publishing the reply under the title, "Censorship and the Future of Asian Theology."[8] In that, he calls 'necro-theology', the theology justifying censorship. Also, in this reply, Kappen distinguishes between the Western and the Eastern ways of thinking and asserts that Jesus was a sun of the Orient and so the Western theologians can never understand him properly.

In his next book *Jesus and Cultural Revolution*,[9] Kappen introduces his notion of Counterculture. Throughout his subsequent writings, we can see him further developing his countercultural perspectives. To him, the anti-Brahmanical movements, beginning with the Buddhist, were examples of Countercultural Movements in India. Later on, he finds fault with the Indian Communists for not taking such movements seriously.

In 1986, Kappen's next book *Liberation Theology and Marxism*[10] was published. He calls the theology that he proposes as 'a theology of integral freedom'. In this book, we can see many philosophical speculations on human's ethical dimension and historical destiny. The Vatican had released two documents attacking Liberation Theologians for their 'flirtation with Marxism.' The essay, "Church, Liberation Theology and Marxism"[11] is a sharp repudiation of the Vatican's charges.

In 1992, came out Kappen's book, *The Future of Socialism and Socialism of the Future*.[12] In this, he envisages a strategy for the socialist transformation of India through a revolution from below, not imposed from above, as in the Soviet Union or China. He redefines class struggle to include the caste struggle and other protest movements and calls the new form of socialist revolution as Trans-class Struggle.[13]

The Last Decade

In the beginning of the last decade of his life, Kappen wrote the aforementioned poem 'What the Thunder Says.' That poem signals a shift in his overall perspectives, with greater emphasis on ecology. For a certain period, Kappen became obsessed with the idea of doing paintings, and he created around 20 paintings, almost all with ecological significance.

Kappen's last essay, "Spirituality in the New Age of Re-colonization"[14], was completed on his last day on earth. This essay contains all his main concerns in an abridged form, and hence I prefer to call it Kappen's Manifesto. In this, for the first time, he refers to the Christian God as Ungod. He replaces the word God with 'the Divine' and elaborates on the ways in which it reveals itself to us.

Now, I remember a seminar, organized by M G University in Kerala in 1980s. There Kappen was asked whether he believed in God. This was his answer, "I don't believe in an almighty God who created the world. But when I hear the cry of the poor and the downtrodden, my heart is filled with compassion. The source of that compassion I call God." It is that God which Kappen renames the Divine, in his manifesto.

Let me recollect another instance. Once, Kappen gifted me with a new copy of Marx's *Grundrisse*. On the first page he wrote, "O! Thou, the Unutterable! Lead me kindly from Light to Darkness." Yes, that is the Divine of Kappen. We can experience the Divine not in the light of known concepts. We can respond to it, but cannot explain in words, for it is un-utterable, beyond words. In this sense, the Divine is a part of 'the Real' of Jacque Lacan. In the Preface of the book, *Liberation Theology and Marxism* Kappen says,

> "The liberation of humans involves at the same time the liberation
> of the Divine from the prison-house of dogma."[15]

Thus, by the end of his life, Kappen liberated himself from Christian Theology. Another thing I have noticed is that he got fascinated by the thoughts of the famous psychoanalyst, Jacques Lacan, especially his notion of the symbolic order. Kappen calls it the symbolic universe, the realm of symbols, myths, metaphors, narratives, and so on that envelops each of us making part of the Unconscious. I remember Kappen advising me to read Lacan before I finished the book I had been writing on Freud. Always refreshed with the latest intellectual developments, Kappen has made original contributions to Marxism, Ecosophy, and Aesthetics.

Kappen and Žižek

Let me conclude this chapter pointing out certain similarities between Sebastian Kappen and Slavoj Žižek, a contemporary philosopher and follower of Lacan. Both are fierce critics of global capitalism and think that Marxism and Christianity can be reinterpreted for the fight against it. Also, both are influenced by Hegelian dialectic. In the critique of Christianity, both of them take different paths but eventually come to almost the same conclusions.

Notes

1. Vol.5, Part 1.
2. Vol. 6, Part 1.
3. Vol. 2, Part 1.
4. Vol. 2, Chapters 7 - 12.
5. Vol.6, Chap.16.
6. Vol.5, Chap.19.
7. Vol.1, Part 1.
8. Vol.1, Chap.26.
9. Vol.3, Part 1.
10. Vol.4, Part 1.
11. Vol.4, Chap.6.
12. Vol.6, Chap.15.
13. Vol.6, p.192.
14. Vol.6, Chap.11.
15. Vol.4, p.4.

2

Marx beyond Marxism

Marx beyond Marxism[1] is the title of an anthology of Kappen's writings on the philosophies of Hegel and Marx. Going through this book, we can see how Kappen liberates Marx from dogmatic Marxism.

Hegelian Dialectics

Hegel's philosophy is qualified as dialectical. The word dialectic is derived from the word 'dialogue.' In a dialogue, the initial proposition (thesis) is negated by another proposition (antithesis). At the end of the ensuing arguments, both sides reach a conclusion (synthesis). In a true synthesis, truths on both sides will be preserved and the untruths eliminated. Any process similar to this is called dialectic or a dialectical process.

To Hegel, nature and each part of it are constantly in a dialectical process. In the beginning, the Idea negated itself and turned into Nature. It is like my idea of a house turning into a visible building built with human labour. Nature goes on dialectically evolving to become finally the Spirit. At a particular stage in this cosmic drama, human beings come to the stage. This new being is the first one endowed with self-consciousness, 'the unity of the individual, and the universal.'[2] In other words, each human is nature become conscious of itself. In the human, Hegel sees the Spirit, the ultimate end-point, in its germinal form and calls it Subjective spirit.

Humans work together producing both mental and physical products out of materials taken from Nature. Hegel gives priority to the mental over physical labour. Among the mental products, family, morality, civil society, and the state together form the Objective Spirit. From the dialectical conflict between the Subjective and the Objective spirits, the next stages, art, religion, and philosophy emerge. This cosmic dialectical dance culminates in the Spirit. This is Hegelian dialectics in a nutshell.

In this Hegelian scheme, from within every phenomenon emerges its negation. This is called the principle of negativity. Later we can see Kappen using this principle in explaining prophecy.

From Hegel to Marx

Marx welcomes the Hegelian scheme for its dynamic world view and the priority given to the subjective role of humans in the dialectical process of Nature and history. But he cannot accept the notion of the Idea preceding and dominating over humans. So, from the whole dialectical movement, he cuts off the Idea and the Spirit that are essentially the same. To him, Hegel inverted the real relation between ideas and the human world.

In the Marxian philosophy, concrete humans 'with eyes, ears, etc. living in society, in the world, and nature' work together and handle the steering of world history.[3] They fashion products, mental and physical, from Nature and at the same time get fashioned by them. Marx even calls Nature the inorganic body of humans.[4] Work is the essence of humans and the products become their bond with others and society.

Alienation

To go further, the Hegelian notions of objectification and alienation are necessary. The Idea that is not an object negates itself and becomes nature, an object. This is the first example of objectification. Since nature is not essentially an idea, Hegel calls it an alienation of the Idea. Likewise, humans are alienated by their products.

But to Marx, human products as such do not alienate humans. What really alienates humans is the alienated nature of their products. This started happening with private property becoming a ruling principle of social life. First of all, products were expropriated from the producers. They became no more a link between humans. The human way of sharing the surplus products with others came to an end. Humans became not what they *ought to be.* The urge to be what one ought to be is the ethical human dimension in Kappen's perspective, and its negation is alienation.

Humans are supposed to work together, producing and sharing things of use and beauty from nature. This makes each human a *being-with-others.* Thus products mediate between humans. Also our relation to things is mediated by our fellow humans. Hence the material world is something like the extension in time and space of our social existence. But private property disrupts this inter-relatedness of humans, nature and the products of labour.

Human alienation reached its climax in the capitalist mode of production. Products turned into commodities, paving the way for the accumulation of capital, leading to the supremacy of the market. Kappen writes, "Thus work which ought to be an end in itself becomes only a means to an end, the end being a few coins."[5]

Today, in the global capitalist system, due to the mass production of untruths as a means of political power, we are entering the frightening post-truth era.

Disalienation through Revolution

Overcoming alienation is disalienation. Capitalism destroys the social essence of humans by splitting the society mainly into two classes: Capitalists - the owners of productive forces - and the working class. The working masses are the most alienated, exploited, and dehumanized. As and when they become aware of their subhuman condition and the need to fight against it, they turn into the proletariat, the revolutionary class. Taken hold off by the hope of achieving freedom, they will fight against the capitalist mode of production and create a classless society. There, with the common ownership of the forces of production, the State – the alienated form of the social dimension of humans – will wither away. Thus Humans overcome alienation by 'the destruction of the alienated character of the objective world.'[6]

Marxian Materialism

Young Marx was confronted with two opposing world views, materialism, and idealism. In materialism, what is primary is the material nature, determined by chemical, physical, and mechanical laws. Human consciousness is seen as derived from the material world. But in idealism, what is primary is the subject, either human or superhuman as the Idea. The objective world is just another mode of being of the subject. Marx attempts to reach a synthesis of idealism and materialism. To him, genuine materialism is based not on blind natural laws but on 'the social relationship between humans.'[7] Also, the word 'material' stands for the reality of human's socio-historical existence. So, what

Marx's historical materialism propounds is that our ideas and conceptions are determined by our concrete social existence.[8]

Another important point in Marxian philosophy is the dialectic of being and thinking. Being is objectively existing, reality. In materialism, our thoughts are just a reflection of being. Against this, Marx affirms the active, dynamic character of human's relation to nature.[9]

Finally, Marx calls his philosophy naturalism or humanism.

"We see how consistent naturalism or humanism is distinguished from both idealism and materialism, and at the same time constitutes their unifying truth. We see also that only naturalism can comprehend the process of world history."[10]

The Dialectic of Revolution

In Marxism, the forces of production of a society are dialectically related to the relations of production. When the relations of production become an obstacle to the growth of the forces of production, the objective condition for revolution develops. This is the Marxist dialectical formula of revolution. In this, the forces of production form the thesis and the relations of production the antithesis.

Kappen doesn't accept this formula as such. In that, obviously, the growth of the productive forces is accepted uncritically, making its relation to the Productive relations one sided, i.e. non-dialectical. Kappen points out this as the cause of Marxism's failure in addressing the environmental problems.

He suggests a modification for this theory of revolution, taking elements from the *Phenomenology of Hegel*. It starts with polar relations involving thesis and antithesis, renamed as equilibrium, and disequilibrium, respectively. Both interact dialectically leading to the higher equilibrium (synthesis). In this perspective, revolution, the way to the higher equilibrium, is the result of mutual interaction between the productive forces and the relations of production. Kappen thinks of 'this approach as better suited to the analysis of historical processes.'[11]

Marx-Engels Non-duality

For orthodox Marxists, Marx and Engels are essentially the same. They cannot think of any conceptual difference between the two intellectuals. But, Kappen breaks this non-dualistic illusion. Engels' main concern is the dialectics of motion in the material nature. The sixth chapter of his book *Dialectics of Nature* is on Electricity and it starts with the statement, "Electricity, like heat, only in a different way, has also a certain omnipresent character. Hardly any change can occur in the world without it being possible to demonstrate the presence of electrical phenomena."

Also, his three laws of dialectics - quantity changes to quality, opposites interpenetrate, and negation of negation – are far from Marxian dialectics that accords a prominent role for human subjectivity. Kappen points out that Marx in his writings does not use the term dialectical materialism. He says,

> "Engels falls into that crass materialism, which Marx tried to dialectically overcome. This Engelsian materialism turns out to be another version of idealism in which Hegel's Idea is replaced by the dialectical laws of motion."[12]

Here we may note that Slavoj Žižek, the well-known contemporary philosopher, too points out the sharp difference between Marxian Dialectics and the Engelsian Dialectical Materialism. As a more acceptable terminology, he suggests 'Materialist Dialectics' - 'the shift from determinate reflection to reflective determination'[13] - thereby giving primacy to Dialectics.

Marx on God, and Religion

Marxism as a theory about human life has to be evaluated based on our understanding of the human. Being self-conscious, we humans want to be what we *ought to be*, our ethical dimension. Logical truth is the conformity of thought with what is thought about. But the truth about humans is not only logical but also dialectical. So, Kappen associates the truth of any theory, like Marxism, with the ethical dimension of humans. It should tell us not only what *is* but also what *ought to be*. Also, it must itself have a role in the transition from the *is* to the *ought*. The human reality that we experience is both *being* and *becoming*. The experienced reality alters our being, which in turn changes the way we experience reality. Similar is the relation between theory and practice. Thus, 'human reality is in creative tension towards its own future.'[14]

To Marx, God is a product of human imagination to which believers project their true essence. This makes them feel as if they are the slaves of God. But all humans are called to absolute freedom and so faith in God and the realization of freedom are incompatible. This makes it our moral imperative to deny the existence of God. Also, Marx's philosophy of history posits the total perfectibility of the human without God's intervention.

Kappen says that the Marxian postulate of the absolute freedom of humans is only an assumption, not derived from any scientific analysis of human life. Without any reliable evidence, it turns into an act of faith. Thus, 'in declaring man to be his own maker, Marx reinstates, unwittingly, the same Absolute which his atheism sought to demolish.'[15]

Another Marxian postulate is that religious belief is born of economic alienation, and hence with its elimination, humans will be able to realize their true essence that is attributed to God. 'But is the claim sustainable in the light of our global historical experience?' asks Kappen.[16]

Another argument of Marx is that 'the idea of God arises from human's need to explain, legitimate, and compensate for his fractured existence in the sphere of material production.'[17] This means that God is supposed to bridge the gulf between the known and the unknown, and between expectation and fulfilment. In such a God of explanation, humans can find ideological legitimation for all their deeds. On this, Kappen agrees with Marx. Believers use God to explain what they cannot fathom. As soon as the 'mysteries' are cleared by science and technology, they are forced to look for another lacuna in human knowledge. Therefore, what they arrive at is 'a spurious Absolute, external to the world.'[18] The true Absolute that Kappen later calls the Divine is not an explanatory principle situated outside the world, but the depth-dimension of human existence.

> "It is the ultimate meaning of history encountered in the realm of practice. Of this true Absolute, the God of explanation is but a caricature."[19]

Kappen points out that Marx's theory of alienation and its supersession is an attempt to bring out the hidden meaning and ultimate goal of history. This does not make him a believer. For a true believer, the ultimate meaning reveals itself in history, while at the same time transcending it. Humans stand in a dialogical relationship with God in whom they find the final source of all meaning. But Marx sees that in humans themselves. His classless society is "the solution of the riddle of history and knows itself to be this solution."[20]

In any society, the ruling classes or castes manipulate the concept of God and use that to legitimize their authority.

Kappen justifies Marx's violent attack on this God of ideological legitimation. He says,

> "It is his abiding contribution to have unmasked the class character of God in much of popular worship. The same God is very much alive even today where religious leaders are in league with the powers that be. Eliminating him is a prerequisite for complete human emancipation."[21]

Another point that Marx raises against religion is that it provides illusory compensation for human miseries. Faith in the life after death dampens our urge to revolt against injustice. Religious cult becomes a substitute for revolutionary practice. On this point, Kappen does not agree fully with Marx. There have been many religions that emerged as the protest of the masses against the prevailing inhuman social conditions. Such protests in this world, is at the root of the projection of a world of love in the world above. Kappen cites Buddhism as an example from India. Its rise 'signalled the revolt of the masses against caste inequality, priestly domination, and the despotism of rulers.'[22] As another example, Kappen points out the prophetic movements in the Bible with its fierce denunciation of social injustice and political oppression. We can see its culmination in the life of Jesus of Nazareth, who had to pay in blood for his 'protest against the oppressive religious and political structures of his day.'[23] Kappen sees its continuation not in Christianity but in the dissenting Christian movements and sects. One such initiative was the League of the Just that gave birth to the First Communist International!

Notes

1. Vol.2, Part 1.
2. Hegel 1991, p.197.
3. Marx 1975, p.398

4. Ibid, p.328

5. Vol.1, p.246

6. Marx, EW, p. 395

7. Marx, EW, p.381

8. Marx, Capital, Vol.1, 1977, p. 29

9. Marx, "Theses on Feuerbach" in EW, p. 421-422.

10. Marx, EW, p. 389

11. Vol.5, p.128

12. Vol.2, p.114.

13. Žižek 2009

14. Vol.2, p.78.

15. Vol.2, p.80

16. Vol.2, p.80

17. Vol.2, p.80

18. Vol.2, p.80

19. Vol.2, p.80

20. Marx 1963, p.155

21. Vol.2, p.81

22. Vol.2, p.82.

23. Vol.2, p.82.

3

Art and Revolution

This chapter deals mainly with two essays of Kappen, "Art and Social Consciousness"[1], and "Towards a Revolution of Symbols."[2] The first is based on Heidegger and the second is influenced by Jacques Lacan. We shall see how these two great thinkers meet in Kappen's writings.

Art and Artwork

To Heidegger, art is a unique way in which the Being of beings is revealed. So, let us see what he means by Being. Taking a tree as an example, what is its Being? It is all that makes it a tree in a part of nature at a particular time with all its relations with all other beings. No amount of information we collect about it can reveal its Being to us humans. The fact that it is feeding with fruits several squirrels need not be there in our data. Thus Being remains concealed from humans.

There is a folk story in Malayalam: A tree was there on the boundary of two neighbouring kingdoms. The king on one side wanted to cut down that tree. But his counterpart opposed it on the ground that the tree was the abode not only of birds (*paravas*) but also deities (*devas*). At last the tree was cut, but it refused to fall down until the sacrificial killing of the offender's daughter.[3]

It is this awareness of our forebears about the Being of beings that we have lost today. We are concerned about what a thing *is*, but not about the fact that it *is*. Art is that which reveals the Being of beings and truth (*aletheia*) is the revelation of Being. Artist is the one who lets truth happen through his/her artwork. And those who decide to live in its light are co-creators of the artwork. Hence, Kappen says, "the truth of a work of art is often perceived more fully by the viewer than by the artist himself."[4] In this sense, aesthetic experience is an encounter with truth.

Let us take Picasso's artwork, *Guernica* as an example. It is not a source of information about the fascist bombing of the town Guernica, nor is it an object of pleasure. But it reveals the hidden realities of the bombing and makes us sensuously experience the horrors of war. It makes us see things in a new light and live in a new world. By the word 'world', Heidegger means the new light of the work of art and the things as seen in that light. Each artwork causes the 'worlding' of a new world to which we humans are elevated.

Next, let us take an example from a poem, written by Kappen: "What the Thunder Says."[5] If T S Eliot wanted to show 'what the thunder said' in his days, Kappen is trying to tell us what it is saying today. Let me quote just three lines from the poem:

"The whites colonized the Black,
the brain colonized the brawn,
the phallus colonized the *yoni*."[6]

'The whites' stand for the *savarnas* in India and the white races elsewhere, and thus the first line reveals the racial domination prevalent all over the world. The second line, with 'the brain' as a metaphor of science and technology, and the brawn as that of Nature, reveals the technocratic domination. In the third line, the term *yoni* (vagina) is of special significance, as in India there was a time when *yoni-puja* was prevalent. Thus the three lines together as an artwork reveal the truth of the racial-technocratic-patriarchal domination, hidden by the secular-democratic narratives in our symbolic order.

Mere Things, Tools, and Artworks

Heidegger calls everything that *is* a being or a thing. He classifies all things into three categories in relation to humans: mere things, tools, and artworks. For a simple example, consider a dark stone in an isolated bush. From a distance, I may be captivated by its beauty amid flowery herbs. This aesthetic experience makes that stone an artwork to me at that moment. The usage of 'captivated' is significant. It is not my tool since, instead of acting on the stone, I am being acted upon by that - a parallax shift in subjectivity. This is what happens in our encounter with an artwork. It takes hold of us like the *la petit à* (the small other) in Lacan.

Now, suppose I walk up and sit on the same stone. Then to me, it becomes a tool. Everything we make use of is a tool. When I get down and walk away, that stone becomes a mere thing to me.

Of these three categories, tools and mere things are necessary in our daily life. It is out of mere things that we make tools and create artworks. But in the realm of necessity, artworks seem superfluous. To Marx, freedom is realized beyond necessity.

When used for a purpose, artworks turn into tools. Kappen quotes an example from Heidegger: Ordinary shoes can be worn; not so the shoes, painted by Van Gogh, of the peasant girl. Does this mean that the painting has no role in our life?

No. It makes us feel the tediousness and sufferings of peasant life and takes us to their world.

So, every artwork has two components: the material substratum and the world it brings up. These two are parts of two wider categories – the Earth and the World. The world is the light in which a people at a particular stage of history see, interpret, and evaluate reality. The world emerges and disappears. Heidegger coins the verb, 'to world' to denote the emergence of a world. The world of tribal peoples differs from the world of caste society. Kappen says,

> "The Enlightenment in Europe saw the worlding of a new world which today is in full swing."[7]

The Earth is that which carries all that *is*, including the worlds. The world emerges from and within the Earth. All things, out of which a work of art is made, belong to the Earth - colour, wood, stone, tone, sound, bodily movements, and so on. All the things on the Earth tend to conceal themselves from humans. Such dimensions inaccessible to human perception and hence beyond language are called deeper dimensions. I think this Heideggerian conception is very close to the Real of Lacan.

Kappen quotes Heidegger from his *The Origin of the Work of Art*,

> "The world grounds itself on the earth, and the earth permeates the world. But the relation between world and earth does not wither away into an empty unity of opposites, unconcerned with one another. The world, in resting upon the earth, strives to surmount it. As self-opening, it cannot endure anything closed. The earth, however, as sheltering and concealing, tends always to draw the world into itself and keep it there." (Kappen's translation from German.)

In this description, the earth and the world are constantly in oneness and tension. Kappen compares this with the unity-in-tension of the *vac-artha* (*vac* = word, *artha* = meaning) in the introductory verse of Kalidasa's *Raghuvamsa*. This brings to my mind the relation between the signifier and the signified of a sign. Any element of the Earth, as defined above, can be the signifier of a sign and hence its earthly part. And the signified – the spectrum of meanings – is vibrant like the world. An artwork is a sign of signs, each of which is a miniature of the earth-world *unity-in-tension*.

The Humans and the Symbolic Universe

We have seen that every being can be a mere thing, a tool, or an artwork. This is true of a human being also. A slave can be a tool to the master while serving him, and a mere thing while taking rest. A dancer is an artwork while dancing. But there is something that makes us humans stand out among all other beings. In the words of Heidegger, a human is a being for which its Being is a problem. A slave can subjectively – to oneself – be never a tool or a mere thing. That is, a human can at any time choose to be what one is not. In this sense, humans are the only beings that exist. For to exist means, to 'step out' (*existere* in Latin). Always we want to go beyond what we *are* and that is self-transcendence. So, Heidegger calls a human a Dasein (da = there, sein = to be). Every one of us has an urge to be what one *ought to be*.

From the past experiences, we create a new project for the future and live in its light. In this sense, we are living from the future to the present, and this is the anticipatory temporality of humans. To Heidegger, genuine thinking is akin to thanking, adoring, communing, and merging with all that *is*.

A human is a *being-with-others* and a *being-in-the-world*. We always see ourselves as part of a community. A community is a group of people who can commune – communicate intimately - with each other. For this, there should be a common language or languages, in the wider sense of a sign system. It may be verbal, visual, actional, passional, etc., each having its grammar, a set of rules. When we communicate in a language, we are unaware of its rules, since they control our words and deeds from our collective unconscious.

Every being appears to us in the guise of a word and that word takes us to many other things. For example, some 'thing' on the roadside may bring to my mind the word 'stone' and the same word may take me to a saint stoned to death. The related Christian narrative gives a mythical halo to the stone.

A symbol is a sign in which the signifier not only points to but also is one with the signified. For example, "the idol in the temple not only points to a deity but also is itself the deity."[8] Thus the same stone, mentioned above may be an object of worship, a symbol of a deity, to another human. All this because we are living within a sphere of narratives, myths, symbols, and so on. This sphere is Lacan's symbolic order and Kappen calls it the symbolic universe. It contains master signifiers also - sounds or images with no specific meaning but having a tremendous influence on us. The sound *ohm* for the Hindu community is an example.

We are unaware of the functioning of the symbolic universe and its impact on our life and activities, individual and collective. Therefore it is a part of our collective unconscious. Lacan calls it the big Other. So, we are never what we think we are. Consciously, I may be very progressive but unconsciously most retrogressive. To explain this, Žižek quotes the biblical words, 'they do not know what they are doing' and defines ideology as the unconscious influence of the big Other.[9]

Now comes the question: Are we bound to follow the dictates of the big Other? There is another sphere enveloping us and that is the Imaginary. We break the commands of the big Other in our world of imagination, the source of our creativity, and artistic talents. And we know art reveals the Being of beings and lifts us into a new world. This makes us aware of the dehumanizing forces of the world we live in and enables us to envisage a new world. Here lies the artistic dimension of the human and also a closely related prophetic dimension. To Kappen, a prophet is one, taken hold of by the socio-ethical project of what one's society *ought to be*. For the prophet Jesus, the project was the Kingdom of God, and for Marx, it was the Classless Society.

For revolutionary changes in society, new symbols of freedom, self-creation, and hope must be created in the symbolic universe. Such symbols must emerge from the struggle of the masses for a richer and fuller life. Only those who have the courage to dissent can create them. In Kappen's words,

> "The new universe of symbols will be the work of writers, poets, and activists who feel with the masses and are radically honest to the pure urge for creation."[10]

Art and Technology

Just as art, technology also is originally a way of revealing the truth. The word technology is derived from the Greek word *techné*, which is closely related to art (*poiésis*). In the past, humans related with nature as its steward with the help of technology. But today, we treat nature as our slave with technology as an instrument of domination. Elsewhere, Kappen calls the dominance of science 'the epistemic tragedy of enlightenment.'[11]

The truth revealed by science is fabricated, enhancing the domination. In Heidegger's words,

> "The revealing that rules in modern technology is a challenging, which puts to nature the unreasonable demand that it supply energy which can be extracted and stored as such."

He continues,

> "The work of the peasant does not challenge the soil of the field."[12]

This exploitative domination is extended to humans too. Kappen sees its culmination in the concentration camps and gas chambers in Germany, built with 'a sophisticated technology of genocide.'[13]

Kappen notes that, in countries like India, the rural peasant communities still preserve their sense of wholeness and "see a river as a river, not as so much H_2O, but as the source and giver of life and as the symbol of the Divine."[14] He urges the artists to turn to them for inspiration for an art that will inaugurate a new and richer human existence.

Any sort of social, political, or religious domination makes the dominated humans mere things or tools, and it is dehumanization. Similarly, human domination over nature denaturalizes nature.

Art reveals the depth of social degradation and makes us authentic human beings who cannot but take a stand against the forces of dehumanization and denaturalization. This is how art becomes a revolutionary force. It acts on society like the fragrance of a flower. A flower does not exist to radiate fragrance. Similarly, art is not for revolution; art itself is revolution.[15]

Art and Prophecy

In Hegelian dialectics, every being is *becoming*, due to the emergence of its negation, and this is called the principle of negativity, 'the mainspring of historical growth.'[16] Subject to this principle, being nature become self-conscious, we humans too are subject to the principle of negativity, and Kappen sees prophecy as an expression of this principle. In each society at all times, its negation takes the shape of its prophets.

In art, the deepest meaning of human existence takes on a sensuous form. This makes the artist similar to the prophet. The prophet also gives expression to the deepest, the ultimate destiny of a people. For that, they too often resort to sensuous forms. For example, the mode of expression of the prophetic writings in the Bible is poetic. The parables of Jesus are poems.

If prophecy is expressed in conceptual terms, it can appeal only to the mind and to a limited number of people. But, if it takes sensuous form as an artwork, it can appeal to a wider section of the people. Also, it can touch 'the deepest core of the human being, the inward sanctuary of the human from where willing, loving, thinking and deciding emerge.'[17]

Prophecy creates a Utopia, which is the ultimate goal of individual and collective existence, like *mukti* in Hinduism, *nirvana* in Buddhism, and the reign of God in Christianity. It acts as a powerful master signifier in the symbolic universe of the masses. Kappen calls it 'the light in which meanings are grasped, values are perceived, hopes crystallize and norms are framed'[18], the totality of which is culture. Culture and Utopia are dialectically related. A radically new Utopia 'will call for a radical questioning and reinterpretation of the prevailing culture.' Conversely, a radical critique of culture involves a reinterpretation of the Utopia.

Art and the Christians

Christians in India are culturally uprooted. They are a people without a memory, and a past. They 'have exorcised away as something unholy, impure' their deep roots in the collective unconscious. So, for the Indian Christians to be creative in the world of art, they have to undergo a rebirth and a conversion of their sensuousness. Only then can they merge with other people and start vibrating to things and persons. In the absence of this conversion, 'artistic creation takes place only among the dissenters, among the dropouts' for they cannot fit into the existing system.[19]

Notes

1. Vol.6, Chap.7.
2. Vol.6, Chap.3.
3. Vattamattam 2011.
4. Vol.1, p.293.
5. Vol.6, Chap.16.
6. Vol.6, p.210.
7. Vol.6, p.100.
8. Vol.6, p.54.
9. Žižek 1989.
10. Vol.6, p.58.
11. Vol.6, p.3.
12. Heidegger, The Origin.
13. Vol.5, p.65.
14. Vol.6, p.107.
15. Vol.6, p.109.
16. Vol.3, p.57.

17. Vol.6, p.148.
18. Vol.3, p.14.
19. Vol.6, p.150.

4

Ecosophical Importance
of the Vedas

Introduction

"Vedic Orientations for a Relevant Ecosophy"[1] is the title of a paper Kappen presented at a seminar in 1987. He starts the paper with a quotation from the *Manifesto of the Communist Party*. It states that history is the story of class struggles. He agrees with this but disagrees with the uncritical acceptance of the productive forces, as we have seen in chapter 2. Today, the major productive forces are science and technology and that has led our world to the present ecological crisis.

Marxism arose as a protest movement against capitalist modernity. It is science and technology that helped the capitalist class amass wealth and establish their domination over humans and nature. Now, above all forms of class struggle, there is going on a struggle of the whole humanity for survival.

Kappen reads the Vedas in the light, or say darkness, of the impending ecological catastrophe. Before coming to that, let us have some ideas about narratives like the Vedas, the Bible, the Koran, and the epics. Such narratives have a prominent role in our symbolic order in the collective unconscious. They provide building materials for many of the symbols, myths, and master-signifiers.

Narratives, in general, are polyphonic and open to dialogal (I prefer this term to 'dialogical') reading. But organized religions and political powers make them monophonic and closed, like Holy Scriptures. Any dialogue with it is prohibited. As a consequence, our symbolic universe becomes stagnant, making us conservative. But in critical periods, we can re-read such narratives making them more dialogal. Let us have an example.

Take the Biblical narrative of the Exodus. A male god declares a nomadic people as his only chosen people, promises them new land to settle, liberates them from slavery, and leads them to the Promised Land. That is the story. The official Christian theologians have been using this to prove their claim that the Christians are the only chosen people of the only God and to legitimize the crimes of the Church. But in the 19th century, there was a Dalit convert called Poykayil Yohannan in Kerala, who read the Bible in the light of the slave experiences of the Dalits. Then he started talking to his people about a God who stood with the slaves and would liberate them *here* and *now*. Soon he met with strong opposition from the official Church and finally founded his own Church, Prathyaksha Raksha Daiva Sabha (Church of Liberation here and now). Similarly, Kappen rereads the Vedas in the present context.

From Physis to God and then to Reason

In his paper mentioned above, Kappen traces how the ancient holistic worldview, in the west, became degenerated. Here, he draws heavily on Heidegger. The word ecology is derived from the Greek word, *Oikos*, literally meaning home. Nature is our home and we are not pilgrims or tourists here in Nature. In ancient Greek narratives, Nature is *Physis* that means everything that comes into being and ceases to be. It is not static but the processes of emerging and merging, of rising and setting, of life and death, of being and becoming.

Later, with the advent of Christianity, humans began to look at reality from a different perspective - as created things. Nature turned into an object made by the subject God who transferred its subjectivity over nature to humans.

Renaissance replaced the Christian God with Reason. The unity of humans and Nature was replaced by the duality of subject and object. Everything in Nature became a tool, an instrument in the hands of humans. Today the Corona virus may not be a scientific product, but the possibility of producing bio-weapons of its kind, cannot be ruled out. We claim to be in cyberspace. The word cybernetic is from the Greek word *kybernetes* which means pilot or captain. We have been thinking of our being the pilots of the cosmic spacecraft and now realize with a shock that it is sinking.

So, what are we to do? Kappen suggests a 'revolution of consciousness'[2] in which we must free ourselves from the partial, analytic, quantitative view of the world. For this, we have to return to the origins, to the thought-world of our forebears, to their world-understanding and self-understanding.

The Vedic Worldview

Every culture has a matriarchal past characterized by the cult of Mother Goddess, asserts J. J. Bachofen[3]. The discovery of the Indus Valley Civilization in the 1920s, and the subsequent investigations, have proved the prevalence of matriarchy and Mother Goddess cult in the pre-Aryan civilization in the Indian subcontinent. Kappen identifies this period as the deepest layer of Indian civilization. Agriculture, the main mode of production in which women took the leading role was then the economic factor behind the pre-eminence of the Mother-Goddess cult.

In this early stage of development, humans found themselves thrown into the midst of inexorable cosmic forces. It is only natural that they saw the Divine in every mysterious object. 'Of all things what appeared most enigmatic to our forebears, was the process of conceiving and giving birth, of which women held the secret.'[4] Hence, there evolved the cult of Mother Goddess.

The economic factor, such as the change over from hoe to plough cultivation, together with the invasion of the patriarchal Aryans, brought about the transition from matriarchy to patriarchy. But elements of the Mother Goddess cult still persist in our society.

The Vedas, in general, reflect the Aryan patriarchal view of the world, and usually, the Brahmanical scholars concentrate on that. But Kappen delineates a matricentric conception of the world in the Vedas, probably assimilated by the Aryans from pre-Aryan matriarchal civilization. This matricentric tradition is centred on the unity of humans and Nature. Kappen wants us to 'go beyond both patriarchy and matriarchy and create a new, androgynous civilization.'[5] Also, to the Vedic people, Nature (*Prakriti*) was the very source of life. In Atharva Veda, there is a prayer for the sick. They pray:

> May the wind breathe
> Purification upon the sick,
> The waters rain immortality,
> The sun warm the body.
> Death show mercy. (AV XII; VE, p.588, verse 5)

There is another *sukta* affirming that we humans have the same fragrance as that of the horses, wild beasts, and elephants. And the Vedic humans pray:

> "O earth, steep us, too, deeply in your fragrance,
> And let no enemy ever wish us ill!"
> (AV XII; VE, p.125, verse 25)

The Vedic people ask mother Earth to impart to them the vitalizing forces from deep within her body, her navel, and to purify them wholly. (VE, p.124, verse 12). The Earth is concerned equally about all the beings she carries. She carries in her lap 'the foolish and the wise. She bears the death of the wicked as well as the good. She lives in friendly collaboration with the boar and offers herself as a sanctuary to the wild pig.' (VE, p.128, verse 48). Also, she shows no discrimination based on caste, colour, or tribe. She 'bears mankind, each different grouping maintaining its own customs and its speech.' To such a mother the Vedic people are praying to 'yield up for them a thousand streams of treasure, like a placid cow that never resists the hand.' (VE, p.127, verse 45). Here, this cow is one that would never allow killing anyone in its name.

The Earth is the abode into which we return on dying. What she has brought forth she takes back. Here is a Rig-vedic funeral hymn:

> Subside into the lap of the Earth,
> Your mother,
> This Earth wide-spreading,
> This kind and gracious maiden
> Who is soft as wool to the generous giver!
> From the womb of Nothingness

May she preserve you!

Make a vault, O Earth;

Do not press down upon him!

Grant him easy access.

Afford him shelter.

Cover him with the skirt of your robe

Just as a mother envelops the child.

(RV X 18; VE, p.610, verse 10)

So, death is not a return to the womb of Nothingness for before the birth we were there as part of the Earth and so will we be after death too. This is why to the Vedic people, every being in Nature was sacred. To them, cultivation was also cult, an act of worship. They never allowed their labour to make the earth sterile. They worked adhering to the cosmic *Rita*, the law governing all processes like the cycle of seasons. The same cosmic *Rita* became ethical behaviour in humans. Later on, Kappen says, it was replaced by dharma understood as *varnashrama-dharma*. The Vedic people knew that all labour not in harmony with *Rita* was an act of violence done to mother Earth. Hence they prayed to her:

Whatever I dig up of you, O earth,

May you of that have quick replenishment!

O purifying One, may my thrust never

Reach right unto your vital points, your heart!

(AV XII, 1; VE, p.126, verse 35)

The human community is connected with the earth with an invisible umbilical cord, like an embryo to the mother. For the embryo to be born, the cord has to be cut off. But in the case of humanity, cutting the umbilical cord will lead to its death. So we are bound to remain not yet born till the end-time. In Kappen's words,

> "The humankind, therefore, is doomed to perpetual embryonic existence….Marx said the same thing when he wrote that nature is man's material and spiritual inorganic body. Nature is not what humans *have* but what they *are*."[6]

To the Vedic people, the whole cosmos was divided into the Macrocosm and the Microcosm. Each part of the first was identical with a corresponding part of the second: the cosmic community with the human community; the light of the sun with the light of the human eye; the wind with human breath; the waters with the vital sap of trees, and the blood and semen of human beings; the regions with human ears; the moon with the mind, and the earth with the human body. (BU III, 2, 10-13; AV VIII, 2). This shows that they saw a magico-religious identity – an *Advaita* - between humans and nature. This original cosmic *Advaita* was, over time, reduced into the metaphysical identification of the individual *Atman* with the *Brahman* (*Aham Brahmasmi*).

Next, Kappen comes to *Kama* (desire) in the Vedas. It was the driving force behind all the striving of the Vedic community. A Rigvedic hymn proclaims, "In the beginning desire arose which was the primal germ-cell of the mind" (X, 129). In the Atharva Veda, it is the firstborn, loftier than the Gods, and humans. (AV IX, 2; VE, p.243, verse 19). Who are the gods in the Vedas? They are no metaphysical beings beyond nature. They lived and interacted with the people helping in their confrontations with the inimical forces of nature.

This primordial cosmic desire becomes human desire binding them into a community. The *Kama* shows its face in many forms of goodness, virtue. So, the Vedic human prays to the *Kama* 'to penetrate within their hearts and send elsewhere all malice!' (AV IX; VE, p.244, verse 25)

Look at another Sukta:
"From desire springs desire,
Leaps from heart to heart.
The mind of my people,
Let that mind be mine!"
(AV XIX, 52: VE, p.245).

In later interpretations, *kama* was reduced to sexual longing, one of the three obstacles to achieving *moksha* (liberation), the other two being *moha* (delusion), and *dvesha* (hate). Also, liberation was reduced to liberation from life on earth.

Next comes *dana* (giving away) in the Vedas. Kappen compares it with *Agape*, the self-giving love. That too is a manifestation of *kama* that reveals itself in every virtue. Kappen cites several quotes about *dana* from the *Rig Veda*. Let us go through a few of them:

Say not, "This poor man's hunger is a
Heaven-sent doom."
To the well-fed, too,
Comes death in many forms.
Yet the wealth of the generous giver
Never dwindles
While he who refuses to give
Will evoke no pity!
....
He who shares not his food with a friend,
The comrade at his side, is no true friend!

From such a one withdraw - no real home his!
Stranger though he be, receive from another!
In vain the foolish man accumulates food.
I tell you truly, it will be his downfall!
He gathers to himself
Neither friend nor comrade.
Alone he eats; alone he sits in sin.
(RV X, 117; VE, 850-851)

The Ecological Relevance of the Vedas

The Vedas provide three corrective principles to overcome the ecological crisis: the holistic, the matricentric, and the erotic-agapic.

The holistic principle

The analytic approach of modern science failed in comprehending realities in their wholeness. Any definition of a reality reduces that into some of its components. When we say that water is H_2O, we are reducing a multidimensional phenomenon into a minute molecule. But to the Vedic people, water was not just one substance among other things; it was also the origin of everything, the source of life and death.

The harmful consequences of the analytical method are quite evident in Modern Medicine. Our body is maintained by the combined efforts of trillions of microorganisms. Without bothering about them, we resort to antibiotic medication, killing many of them along with the inimical ones. This is like burning the house to kill a rat.

Kappen proposes that we must make modern science subservient, and be guided by the holistic view of the universe that prevailed in Vedic times. It must do justice to the interrelatedness of all things. Here, I am reminded of the following folksong of the Paraya community in Kerala:

> The Earth of which I came out,
> The Earth in which I was,
> May Earth unite with Earth,
> May Quarters (*dik*) unite with Quarters,
> May land (*desam*) unite with land,
> May the unknown (*mayam*) unite with the unknown.
> May the dead (*chav*) unite (with me)
> May my father unite (with me),
> May my mother unite (with me)
> May my sisters unite (with me)
> May Earth shine in unison with Earth,
> May Quarters shine in unison with Quarters,
> May land shine in unison with land,
> The gods shall shine on that land.[7]

So, to the Parayas, all the beings including Gods were interrelated.

The matricentric principle

It is the patriarchal Judeo-Christian God who enjoined on humans "to fill the earth and subdue it." (Genesis 1:28). Kappen considers this command as a major factor that contributed to the development of science, technology, and industrialization with its concomitant ecological devastation. Kappen qualifies as matricentric the Earth-centered conception of the world, evident in the Vedas. Our kinship with nature is characteristic of this matricentric conception, and we have to make a conscious effort to recapture it. This involves dismantling all technology and industrialization that does violence to the earth.[8]

The erotic-agapic principle

As seen already, *Kama* is a cosmic force that in human beings is the longing for the fullness of having and being and the spontaneous straining toward the good and the beautiful. It might appear today that modern science and technology have enhanced the possibility of satisfying human desires. But Kappen says,

> "In truth, technocratic, consumerist society has only rendered human desires stereotyped and standardized to suit the needs of production for profit. In the process, authentic desire, including sexual desire, is repressed and human existence impoverished."[9]

So we have to return to the Vedic understanding of *kama* as the community's longing for human cosmic plenitude. With the emergence of private property and the *varna* system, *Kama* was debased to the desire for one's happiness. It was to counter the rising individualism that the Upanishads and the Buddha projected the ideal of *nish-kama-karma* (action without desire). What it means is that our actions should be without selfish desire. With the disintegration of tribal solidarity and the emergence of private property, the ideal of *dana* was degraded. We have to restore *kama* and *dana* in the Vedic sense. For this to be possible 'we must break loose from the rule of private property, the techno-centric engineering of consciousness and all repressive state apparatuses.' Also, Kappen proposes the emergence of new communities 'based not only on the collective decision but also, and above all, on the understanding of nature as our common home (*Oikos*) and our common Mother.'[10]

Notes

1. Vol.6, Chap.5.
2. Vol.6, p.74.
3. Bachofen 1967.

4. Vol.5, p.4.

5. Vol.6, p.75.

6. Vol.6, p.80.

7. Vattamattam, Chapter 6, in Madhusoodanan(2022).

8. Vol.6, p.88.

9. Vol.6, p.88.

10. Vol.6, p.89.

5

Counterculture and
the Revolution of Symbols

As we have seen already, Kappen identifies the present era as the age of re-colonization in which humans and nature are colonized by global capitalism. This unholy world order is supported by atomic weapons provided by Science and Technology. Kappen proposes a counterculture, and a revolution of symbols.

Culture and Cultural Paradigm

A community is a social formation in which the members can commune with each other in a common language. Such a language is based on mutual understanding and faith. Since words can have different meanings, there is no guarantee that I am saying what you understand and you understand what I mean. It is a matter of faith between you and me uniting us into a 'we.' Thus Kappen describes culture as "the organic whole of ideas, beliefs, values, and goals which condition the thinking and acting of a community or people."[1]

Culture is expressed in ethics, philosophy, law, art, literature, myth, conventions and so on. Also it is expressed in all the institutions. Here Kappen distances himself from the Marxist notion of culture as the superstructure of society with the economic infrastructure. Also we can see that culture, as understood by Kappen is rooted in the collective unconscious of the society, as part of the symbolic universe.

Another related notion of Kappen is the cultural paradigm. In a certain period of time, a people may have a common pattern of seeing themselves, others, and the other beings, and that is their cultural paradigm of that period. For an example, let us take orientalism of Edward Said. During the colonial period, the West constructed an image of the East as uncivilized, and economically stagnant, but at the same time spiritually superior. It was like making a mirror with an uneven surface that distorts the image. Looking in that Western mirror, we the Orientals thought we were what we saw in it. This is orientalism as a cultural paradigm and decolonization is an attempt to liberate ourselves from that, somewhat like a child's transcending the mirror stage, realizing its otherness from its mirror image (Lacan).

Re-colonization of the World

I remember, once in the past our Indian finance minister visiting the United States. There, welcoming the American investors to India, he made a public statement that India's fertile womb was open to them. The news of that shameless declaration elicited vociferous protest from all over India. But today, we find our country and the rest of the world in the womb of global capitalism.

This parallax shift corresponds to a paradigm shift. At least the ruling classes in India and abroad fall into the same pattern of thinking, the scientific paradigm as Kappen calls it. In this, scientific Reason is the God almighty. It makes us approach anything analytically, intervening in smaller parts of entities unconcerned about its impact on the whole; forgetting the wholeness of beings. To us humans, everything appears as fragments, resulting in the fragmentation of consciousness. We are losing our sense of continuity in time and space with others and nature.

Another consequence of the new paradigm is the well-known Cartesian dualism. We think of ourselves as the only thinking beings (*ego cogitans*) and all the rest as extended matter (*res extensa*). Kappen suggests 'machine' as the root metaphor of this scientific paradigm. We think of everything including ourselves as a machine.

Another characteristic of the scientific paradigm is that it doesn't accept anything metaphysical, beyond matter. But Kappen asserts that modern science itself is metaphysical. An example from Heidegger: Newton's first law of motion states: "Every body, left to itself, moves uniformly in a straight line." In the whole universe, is there anything left to itself, not acted upon by any force? No. So, it is only a metaphysical postulate.

Science determines our way of thinking and being. But today science almighty itself is under the control of Global capitalism. This is what Kappen calls the Monotheism of Capital, subserved by Reason. Capital is the only God and World Market is its Church. The Promised Land is that of endless consumption. The Christian motto, 'No salvation outside the Church' is replaced by, 'No salvation outside the Market.'[2] Many of the organized religions have been absorbed into this new religion, promoting re-colonization and engaging in the fast flourishing spiritual industry.

Today, in the global capitalist system, with its development project, determined by market rationality, parts of nature and ever increasing number of humans are turned into mere garbage and thrown out. Due to the Covid 19 pandemic, when lockdown was declared in India, we witnessed thousands of migrant labourers crowding through the streets of Delhi, surrounded by multi-storeyed buildings. The whole scene can be taken as a miniature of the global capitalist world today. The buildings symbolize the chosen people of the almighty Capital, and the flooding river of humans, the living human garbage.

Classless Society and Counterculture

It was in the early period of competitive capitalism that Karl Marx came up with the utopia of a classless society. Kappen summarizes its salient features: In the classless society, there will be common control over material and cultural production, and distribution; the product of labour will be the bond of love between the humans; the greatest need of a human will be the need for fellow humans; freedom will be realized more in the creation of the beautiful than in production of the useful. It will be "an age in which humans, bonded by concern for common good and commitment to the creation of beauty, will collectively shape their own future."[3]

To Kappen, the utopia of a classless society remains an ever receding horizon of hope, an eternal challenge for humans to realize. For its realization, we must liberate ourselves from the scientific paradigm and embrace a new holistic paradigm. In this new paradigm, we must respect the wholeness and the holiness of the universe; see everything in its overall context, because the parts can be known only in the light of the whole. Kappen proposes dance, like the cosmic dance of Siva, as the root metaphor of the holistic paradigm.[4] To achieve all this, the existing culture has to be subverted and a new culture created. This revolutionary process is what Kappen calls counterculture.

The symbolic universe plays a substantial role in the formation of our subjectivity. Its norms and values are filtered down to the masses through cultural organizations and institutions like the family, the caste, the temple, the school, and the media and so on. They produce the kind of humans necessary for the society, by instilling in them appropriate reflexes, attitudes, values, and ideas.

> "Hence no social revolution is possible without radically transforming these institutions and organizations in such wise that they become vehicles of a counterculture."[5]

It should be able to subvert the existing cultural paradigm and create a new one.

The Holistic Paradigm

In many of his writings, Kappen has elicited the reasons for the failure of the Communist movement in realizing the socialist utopia of a classless society. One of them is the negligence of the cultural ecosystem, as a result of the economic determinism that asserts the primacy of the economic infrastructure of the society. Kappen asserts that political, ethical, aesthetic and religious dimensions of life are primordial and not derivative. These dimensions, and the values pertaining to them, must broadly inform the political, economic, and cultural life and structures.

Another reason is the uncritical acceptance of the productive forces, leading to the ecological crises. As a consequence, the communist movement succumbed to the scientific paradigm of global capitalism.

So, for the realization of the socialist utopia, Kappen proposes a new holistic cultural paradigm. We have to accept that it is the whole of any reality that makes its parts intelligible and the whole cannot be mastered by human mind. We must accept the non-duality of the subject and the object and recognize the mystery of the universe. The goal of knowledge in the scientific paradigm is control over nature. But in the holistic paradigm, it should be communion with nature.

From the Indian history, Kappen points out the Buddhist movement as an example of counterculture. The Buddha's thinking was dialectical as in Marx. He spread his new vision through dialogues with his followers. He called upon each of them to be 'a lamp unto oneself', which is in resonance with Marx's words that 'each human must move around oneself as one's own sun.' Also, the Buddha was the first to pose the problem of human alienation and to point out the economic basis of violence. He was the first to start a radical critique of religion, ritualism and superstitions; to repudiate caste inequality and discrimination; to envision the disappearance of the State and project a future reign of justice. The Buddha shifted the axis of religiosity from human-nature relationship to inter-human relations. Also, he instructed the Bhikkus to refrain from all magical practices and offerings to Gods and Goddesses.

Kappen finds the signs of emerging countercultural movements in the struggles of the deprived and the marginalized – adivasis, dalits, women and so on and in the ongoing ecological and antinuclear movements. It should be accompanied by a revolution of symbols.

> "Tomorrow's will have to be symbols not only of fate but of freedom, not of blind conformity but of self-creation, not merely of resignation but also of hope."[6]

Notes

1. Vol.3, p.5.
2. Vol.6, p.120.
3. Vol.6, p.135.
4. Vol.6, p.93.
5. Vol.2, p.176.
6. Vol.6, 58.

6

God, Ungod, and the Divine

This chapter is mainly based on Fr. Kappen's last article, 'Spirituality in the New Age of Re-colonization.'[1] Having finished writing this article by noon, he went for a nap, had a cardiac arrest and was taken to hospital where he returned to the mother earth.

Before coming to Kappen's thoughts, let me share with you what I think of God. God is a powerful master signifier in the symbolic order of any community. The very sound of the word God or an equivalent term can create vibrations in our whole being. This may happen also to one who resolutely denies the existence of God. One is likely to be haunted by God as something that has to be driven out. In the 1970s, I, then a confirmed atheist, came across the 'Death of God Theology.' I still remember how enthusiastically I read writings related to that for I wanted the God haunting me to be dead.

Now, what is the rationale behind the persistence of God in our minds? We all had an infantile experience which Freud calls oceanic experience. It is what we experienced in the womb or lap of the mother before the weaning time – a sense of perfect protection, peacefulness, happiness and oneness with the whole, the mother. This experience is beyond words and hence remains as a part of the Real - all that is beyond the linguistic expression - of Lacan. Its memory remains instilling in us the desire for perfection, and the spirit of self-transcendence.

I think, God in our symbolic order is a projection of this oceanic experience. This explains Freud's contention that religious experience like *Samadhi* is a mental regression to the oceanic experience.

If God is rooted in such a personal experience, what is behind the sense of solidarity of the believers? Here I think we should go to our collective experience of the oneness with the tribe in the tribal period – a time when we were not yet born as individuals. We experienced perfect safety within the tribe and were ready to fight unto death for its survival. Religious solidarity must be having its roots in this tribal life experience.

Religions attempt to symbolize and conceptualize God – to give *nama* and *roopa* to the unspeakable and invisible. Look at any Hindu temple in Kerala. Before it was built, in its place there was only a stone at the bottom of a tree, and now that location is called *moola sthanam*. That stone was probably the first attempt to symbolize the God in the symbolic order. If so, the present temple stands for the later conceptual accumulations added to the original stone symbol of God.

Islam is a religion that is opposed to the making of any image of their God. But if they kill those who do it, then they are making an image of their God as the most intolerant.

God and the Ungod

God is often used as a means of political power. In the old testament of the Bible, God commands humans to subdue the earth. Christianity extended that to subduing the Divine as well.

To Kappen, the Cross is the supreme symbol of human's *no* to all forms of domination. Medieval Christians recast it into 'a sword and wielded it to massacre not less than two million Turks during the Crusades.'[2]

The God of the rich is a product of the priests, religious teachers, theologians, and philosophers, for providing ideological support to the rich. As a product of their labour, God is made a commodity in the spiritual market. Kappen calls this commoditized God a deity.

> "Thus money, the universal equivalent of all commodities, becomes the equivalent of the deity as well. The moneyed can from now on buy the grace (favour) of the deity. They can accumulate religious merit by making donations to religious institutions and by having religious services held for the salvation of their souls. Not compelled to work in order to make a living, they have plenty of leisure to visit shrines and go on pilgrimages. They can indulge both in conspicuous consumption and in spiritual consumption. Thus the economically privileged become also the spiritually privileged."[3]

Consequently, there developed a religious attitude to money and a monetary attitude to religion. Kappen finds the symbolic expression of this assimilation and fusion of money and the deity in the images of the deity made of precious metals.

Kappen begins the essay mentioned above, comparing two utopias: The kingdom of God of Jesus and the Socialist Utopia of Marx. The first degenerated with the emergence of Christianity as a monarchical institution and the second with the emergence of the Soviet Union as a totalitarian regime. Kappen expresses the hope that the socialist utopia will never perish.

To Kappen, Biblical narratives are predominantly symbolic. For example take: "He (Jesus) saw the heavens torn open and the spirit, like a dove, descending upon him."(Mark 1:10) Traditionally, Christianity takes 'the spirit' as the third in the three-in-one Holy Trinity. But to Kappen, it is only a symbol of the power of God. Even the picture of God as father, we get from this story, is derived from 'a patriarchal view of the world where the father is supreme as the source of power, order, and discipline.' Kappen writes:

> "Today we are witnessing the collapse of patriarchal civilization. Motherhood is once again coming to the fore: motherhood of the woman, of the earth, of the waters. And motherhood is the matrix of unconditional love and compassion, and the source of the sense of the equality of all."[4]

These words foreshadow his later vision of God, as Mother Earth and as the Divine.

In a society divided on the basis of caste, colour, class or ethnicity, God is made into concepts that justify the power of the powerful and pacify the powerless. It is this God that Kappen calls the Ungod in his last essay.

Global Capitalism and the Ungod

Next to atomic weapons, it is the Christian God that has contributed to the growth of global capitalism and still provides it with ideological support. Kappen calls it the Christian Ungod. It is a God that legitimizes the lust of Christianity for wealth and power. In the past, this Ungod instigated the Crusades; encouraged inquisitions; authorized the Christian Kings to colonize all the 'pagan' nations; gave the green signal to slave trade. Now it takes the side of the affluent against the poor, of the powerful against the weak. "Its hands are dripping with the blood of the innocent." It is 'a guardian of genital morality, but unconcerned about the immorality of exploitation and injustice.'[5]

The traditional mode of thinking in the West is representational. It extracts the essence from the existents, and form concepts meant to represent reality. It is also analytical, dissecting the real into its constituent elements, and it disrupts the unity of being and knowing. This technological approach has the goal of establishing domination over the whole world, and gaining mastery over the earth. Knowledge thus becomes a means to power. Kappen says,

> "Thinking, rooted in and spurred on by the will to power, ends up by becoming an instrument for the domination of human beings, as is borne out by the history of colonialism, fascism, and the on-going technocratic manipulation of the masses."[6]

The Divine

Kappen rejects the anthropomorphic conception of God as a person. Thinking of God as a person makes it difficult to experience God as all-pervasive, as the One who is in everything and in whom everything is. Such a vision was there in India, 'both in the cosmic religion of the masses and the gnostic religion of the elite.'[7]

In the last period of his life, Kappen started thinking of a new term to replace God to avoid its gender and other connotations. Once he told me jokingly of a new choice: shit. I asked him why? He said that the word shit had she, he, and it in it, but it was not she, not he, and not it. Though a joke, it was quite revealing. Kappen wanted a word that didn't imply gender or even a thing. And finally his choice fell on the word Divine. The Divine is not beyond Nature and history. It is unspeakable, defies all defining, and not a thing among things. It can only be encountered or experienced.

The Divine is like what light is to things lighted up. What we see are things lighted up; light itself remains unseen, though not un-experienced. In like manner we encounter the Divine in things, in persons, in the community, and in history. The Divine is the depth-dimension of the world we live in and the world we *are*.[8]

Long back Kappen had written,

"It is in the radiance of the myriad human faces that surround him that each man will discover the face of God as well as his own true visage."[9]

This is true of the Divine too. It is neither personal nor impersonal, not only being but also becoming, reveals itself not only *in* but also *as* nature and history.[10]

Then what is faith? It is openness to the Divine, and like the Divine, it too is not a concept. It can be expressed only in symbols, which, unlike concepts, are multidimensional in meaning. The life of a believer is a symbol of faith. To our forebears, everything - rivers and forests and mountains and earth and sun and moon and stars – was reality and symbol in one. For them, the whole of reality was shot through with the Divine. There is a folksong, a hymn of the Parayas in Kerala that praises everything:

What is there that I shall praise?
Who is there that I shall praise?
In the East, praise the rising sun;
That name, I praise that holy name.
In the West, praise the setting sun;
That name, I praise that holy name.

In the North, praise the *Maveli*;
That name, I praise that holy name.
In the South, praise the *Theveli*;
That name, I praise that holy name.
In the High, praise the sky above;
That name, I praise that holy name.
In the Low, praise the earth below;
That name, I praise that holy name.
What then is there I shall praise?
Who then is there I shall praise?
The people of this land I praise
The people that have come I praise.

(*Maveli*: a mythical benevolent ruler; *Theveli*: *Sree-devi*, an ancient Mother Goddess)[11]

This is one of the hymns chanted at the beginning of the folk arts such as *Mudiyattam* (hair-dance), and *Kolam-thullal* (mask-dance). For the primal people, there was nothing on earth that was not a symbol of the Divine and hence worthy of being praised. Kappen asks a very relevant question,

> "How can you violate nature, when you know that divinity runs through her veins?"[12]

Alienation of Faith

There are many ways in which faith is alienated. One is *reification*. In Marxist literature, we read about the reification of commodities. It happens when a product of human labour loses its unique use value and made into a commodity, that can be exchanged for any other commodity. Similarly, when unspeakable Divine is translated into concepts, it turns into knowledge that is manageable for the production of power.

Just as humans use science to gain power over nature, they use theology to master the Divine. This is what Kappen calls the reification of the Divine.[13]

Another factor that alienates faith is religious law. To Kappen, true faith knows only one law, that of love. But religions are organized on the basis of numerous human-made laws, proclaimed as God-given. A striking example is the Canon law of the Catholic Church. The Church hierarchy projects its will as the will of God, and silences the Divine with the canon law.

"Thus faith itself became an instrument of repression."[14]

Theandric Practice

Like the Idea and the Universe in Hegelian dialectics, Kappen thinks of the world as moving forward in continuous dialogue between the Divine and humans, and he calls it Theandric practice. He writes,

> "What is history but the transcendence of God become the self-transcendence of human beings through project and *praxis*? It is the unconditional call of the Divine which enables us to break loose from the ever-rotating wheel of cyclic time and march forward to the horizon of human-divine fullness, despite reverses and regressions."[15]

We encounter the Divine in the *here* and *now* of history in two ways: as a gift and a challenge.

The Divine as a Gift

As a gift, we experience the Divine in all our pleasant experiences, and new possibilities of being and becoming. We experience it in 'the soothing, enlivening, sustaining ambience of mother Earth', in the ways in which she communicates with us - through the whistle of the wind, the song of birds and the rustle of leaves and the chant of the oceans. The Divine pulsates in *Kama*, the telluric desire. It reveals itself in the two-in-oneness of sexual love, in friendship and the communion of shared hope and struggle, in the love that gives and in giving replenishes itself, and in works of art - the sensuous revelation of being. The Divine becomes en-fleshed as the desire of humans for the plenitude of being. It is also enfleshed in nature, conscious and unconscious.

"The earth is the symbol and abode of the Divine."[16]

The Divine as a Challenge

We experience the Divine as a challenge to preserve the divine gift as a whole; to strive to realize it ever more fully; to share the divinely given with our fellow humans; to fight against situations where the integrity of the earth is threatened or the human is trampled upon; to fight against every form of injustice and domination; to get involved in transformative practice that humanizes the face of the earth.

In this perspective, we can see the divine revealed in the life of all the revolutionaries fighting against unjust socio-political structures. We ordinary people also must have experienced the divine many a time in life. In this pandemic period, we daily see many people, prepared even to die for serving fellow humans. Now reading Kappen, we know that they are in the grip of the Divine, whether they believe in God or not.

Kappen sees the Divine in 'the emergent struggles of the deprived and the marginalized like Aborigines, Dalits, Tribals and Women' and in the 'on-going ecological and anti-nuclear movements.' In such struggles, the Divine *no* to evil is operative in the *here* and *now* of history. Kappen says,

> "Meeting the Divine as a challenge will initiate a new liberative and creative *praxis* that is non-sectarian, inter-religious, and truly ecumenical."[17]

In the Marxian spirit, Kappen asserts that the truth of our claims has to be verified on the basis of their ability to change the world. This is true of our faith in God too.

> "To proclaim God from housetops carries little conviction if we ignore the God who dwells under leaking roofs."[18]

We must strive to make the new heaven and the new earth a reality.

The Divine challenges us to socialize property, so that both nature and our products become vehicles of human togetherness and each of us becomes *being-for-others*. Also whatever we produce must not only be useful but also beautiful. In our beautiful products Kappen perceives the convergence of the human and the Divine.

> "Only then shall nature cease to be something to be violated and ravished by lust for profit and power."[19]

Discourse on the Divine

In the new light of the Divine, there should be a radical change in the way we speak about the Divine/God. We are used to saying that 'God is love', 'God is truth' and so on. Now, we have to reformulate such statements as 'Love is divine', 'Truth is divine', 'Caring for the widow and the orphan is divine', and so on. In doing so, we are re-joining Gandhi. He wrote that for a long time he used to say, 'God is truth', but subsequently came to realize, he should rather say, 'Truth is God'.[20]

Kappen adds,

> "Tell the slum-dwellers of Bombay or Calcutta, 'God is the defender of the poor' and you are lucky if they don't lay hands

on you. Not so if you tell them, 'when you love one another, when you strive to shake off your shackles you are under the grip of the Divine.'"[21]

Laws, written or not, act on us from outside like an 'other.' They make us depend on mediators like prophets, teachers, and priests. Laws codified at an earlier stage cannot adequately meet the demands of humans' on-going dialogue with the Divine. Therefore, the Law itself can become an obstacle in the way of human's historical self-creation. If so, not only the State, but also the Law needs to be transcended. In the new age, the community will know God in knowing the depths of its own existence.

"This implies further, the death of the God outside-and-above-man."[22]

Here Žižek's book *Monstrosity of Christ*[23] comes to my mind. In it, Žižek re-interprets the biblical narratives about Christ and the Trinity in the light of Hegelian dialectic. After the death of Christ, the father-God transforms through the Son to the Holy Spirit. The Creator of the universe unfolds Himself in the community of believers. There is no longer a hidden God, nor a Son of God, but only the Holy Spirit. That is what is revealed in the early Christian communities of the New Testament, which Engels considers an example of Primitive Communism. Christ says, "When you are gathered in my name, I will be there with you." That 'I' is the Holy Spirit.

Žižek starts with the Christ and the Trinity as produced and propagated by Christianity. But Kappen focuses on Jesus, the self-proclaimed Son of Man, subdued and hidden behind the entire Christian ideological edifice developed in the course of history. Interestingly, both reach almost the same conclusions.

A New Spirituality

Kappen is searching for a new spirituality. He uses this term not in opposition to materialism. It means the way in which we humans go beyond ourselves and reach out to our ultimate possibilities – of being what we ought to be. Now this is prevented by the materialism of consumption promoted by the market.

The new spirituality is one that makes us concerned about the deepest meaning of life and its realization.

> "The Divine does not irrupt into our mindscape from some over world of disembodied spirits but appears to us enfleshed in nature, conscious and unconscious."[24]

It makes us take responsibility for the well-being of all that is. It is not other-worldly, but telluric, earthly. It fills us with the sense of reverence for, and solidarity with, the earth; makes us see in the earth our Mother, the dwelling of the Divine. Our sense of kinship extends beyond family, and humankind, to the universe of animals, plants, planets, and galaxies.

Also, the new spirituality is to be erotic-agapic. That means, it 'reinstates the erotic as the source of creativity, fruitfulness, and communitarian bonding', and love as self-giving. Kappen says that only such a spirituality 'that synthesizes Eros and agape can face the feminist and ecological challenges of today.'[25]

Another aspect of the new spirituality is aesthetic. We have seen that art is the revelation of truth. If truth is the Divine, then art lets it indwell the earth in sensuous form and enable us to communicate it to our fellow humans.

Also, spirituality should be not individualistic but communitarian. The capitalist individualism implies the fragmentation of the social essence of humans, and scientific rationality the fragmentation of human consciousness. Rational and secular thinking makes the present an end in itself, valued in terms of the pleasure it can give. Human existence is thus reduced to a series of disparate experiences of pleasure and pain. This fragmentation thus destroys traditional cultures, and 'focuses on immediate consumption at the cost of humankind's global, future well-being.'[26]

Let me conclude this chapter, quoting Fr. Kappen's last written words:

> "The spirituality adumbrated here must translate itself into action aimed at rolling back the invasion of the consumerist utopia, on the one hand, and realizing the socialist utopia as reinterpreted in the context of post-modernity, on the other."[27]

Notes

1. Vol.6, Chap.11.
2. Vol.5, p.71.
3. Vol.3, p.121.
4. Vol.4, p.125-126.
5. Vol.6, p.137.
6. Vol.1, p.324.
7. Vol.3, p.65.
8. Vol.6, p.130.
9. Vol.1, p.99.
10. Vol.3, p.65.
11. Sebastian Vattamattam, "Biodiversity and Theo diversity" in Madhusoodanan 2022, p.49.
12. Vol.4, p.52.
13. Vol.6, p.131.
14. Vol.6, p.133.

15. Vol.4, p.21.

16. Vol.6, p.143.

17. Vol.6, p.127.

18. Vol.1, p.261.

19. Vol.4, p. 21.

20. *Young India*, 31 December, 1931, pp.427-428.

21. Vol.4, p.42.

22. Vol.1, p.311.

23. Žižek, *Monstrosity.*

24. Vol.6, p.143.

25. Vol.6, p.144.

26. Vol.3, p.186.

27. Vol.6, p.146.

7

Religion and Caste in India

Myth and Religion

As we have seen earlier, humans have an ethical dimension concerning what one ought to be. We experience this as an unending urge to renew ourselves; liberate ourselves from all the limitations and achieve perfection. Every moment, we go on visualizing and hoping for a new future, individually or collectively, better than the present. This is what Kappen calls the depth-dimension or transcendence. This draws us beyond the limits of the immediately given and makes us experience the ultimate horizon of hope as an asymptotic concept, i.e., one that can never be fully realized. It can be expressed only in symbols and myths. Myths appeal to the conscious as well as the unconscious and hence they alone can galvanize humans into action.

> "None will lay down his life for an abstract system of philosophy or dry economic formula. That is why every revolution hitherto has projected its array of myths."[1]

In our day-to-day life, this depth-dimension is only implicitly perceived, as an Other, that inspires us from within or beckons us from beyond. It is this Other that Kappen often refers to as the Absolute or the Divine. We humans have a tendency to symbolize in words or deeds, such implicit perceptions.

> "Thus formulas of faith, as well as rites, rubrics, norms, and institutions, come into being. It is this articulate expression of the depth-dimension of individual and collective life that we traditionally call religion."[2]

Kappen posits religious consciousness or 'religiosity as an original, primordial dimension of human existence and not a by-product of economic alienation', as Marx claims.[3]

Different Types of Religiosity

Cosmic Religiosity

Cosmic religiosity is centred on the cosmic myths about the world above. In India in the Vedic period, it was based on the magical identity of the microcosm with the macrocosm. Humans found themselves entangled in ever-recurring cycles of cosmic phenomena. This instilled in them a cyclic sense of time.[4] The Divine was identified with the cosmic order (*rita*) and humans could influence it by symbolically re-enacting the cosmic cycles.

In cosmic religiosity, natural phenomena, like the sun, the moon, rain, thunder, and so on become objects of worship. The cyclic sense of time makes it basically conservative. It becomes magic when the believer tries to control the Divine through the symbolic, microcosmic presentation of the macrocosm. This possibility leads to the discovery of a magico-religious technology of manipulating the Divine, and the emergence of a priestly class of religious technicians like Brahmanas in India.

Gnostic Religiosity

The religious technicians evolved and propagated what Kappen calls 'gnostic religiosity'. In this, *Brahman,* the macrocosm beyond the world of everyday experience, is the ultimate spiritual ground of all that is. It is at the same time identical with the microcosm, the *Atman,* one's deepest self. Ignorance (*avidya*) of the non-duality (*advaita*) of both is the root cause of all human alienation and suffering. Humans could escape from all the suffering and cycles of birth and death by enlightenment (*jnana*), the knowledge of the *advaita* of *Atman* and *Brahman.*

Personalist Religiosity

In this, the Absolute is perceived as a person who loves and hates, punishes and rewards, creates and redeems. The believer relates to the Absolute through love. The sense of time proper to Personalist religiosity is ecstatic. It collapses the past, the present, and the future into a sort of timelessness. But this is true only of the peak moments of devotional ecstasies. In everyday life, the devotees fall back upon cyclic time as expressed in the cycles of devotional practices. In matters of morality, they tend to conform to the *status quo*, however inhuman it might be. Undergirding this kind of religiosity is the experience of sentimental union with the Absolute. This may infuse some gentleness and compassion to the suffering fellow humans.

Ethical Religiosity of the Buddha

In the course of time, Vedic religion became more and more hierarchical, ritualized and oppressive. At the same time, new productive forces, and the resultant break-up of tribal bonds, made humans aware of their own self-identity. It is at this juncture, that the Buddha came as a prophet of ethical religiosity. He denounced the *varnasrama-dharma* of discrimination and preached the *sanatana dharma* of equality, universal friendliness (*maitri*), and compassion (*karuna*). Buddhism developed into a cultural movement for a genuinely universal ethics.

To Gautama Buddha, *nirvana* is the universal love and central place is given to ethics in its pursuit. It is the ultimate horizon of human existence signalled by the destruction of *raga* (lust), *dvesha* (hate), and *moha* (delusion). As mentioned earlier, the Buddha shifted the axis of religion from man-nature relationship to inter-human relations.

Prophetic Religiosity

Prophetic faith encounters the Divine as one involving in history, and experiences it as a challenge to shake off all shackles and create a future of love, and freedom. It is based on proleptic myths, such as the 'Kingdom of God' of Jesus, and the 'Classless society' of Marx. Such future oriented myths, induces a new sense of time focused on the future yet to be created. This makes the present meaningful as the meeting point of Divine challenge and human response.

Prophetic religiosity is essentially subversive, a catalyst of disequilibrium and a sign of contradiction. It is always in creative tension towards humanity's Absolute Future. That future will eliminate, once and for all, human alienation.

> "Prophetic religiosity signals the birth of something radically new in so far as it entails a new sense of time and an ethics of subversion."[5]

Critique of Brahmanism

Brahmanic religiosity is mainly gnostic. As Kappen observes, it is not an escape but an 'in-scape' from the cyclicity of existence and suffering into the timelessness of samadhi. This makes gnostic religiosity highly individualistic. *Bhagavad Gita* preaches this philosophy: "The wise lament neither for the living nor for the dead."[6]

Gnostic religiosity reduces humans and their life to mere appearance (*maya*), the play of the *nirguna Brahman*. The doctrine of *karma* postulates that each of our deeds in this life will hold us responsible even after death. The retribution takes place through a sequence of rebirths (*punar-janmas*) that involves a movement through numerous life forms. Our experiences in this life are forms of reward or punishment for our actions in the previous life. The total submission to the cosmic laws, as well as the denial of human subjectivity is the essence of the doctrine of *karma*. Kappen makes an interesting observation on how the karma principle persists even today:

> "*Karma* reappears under the guise of the necessary laws of international economy, which dictates the living conditions of individuals."[7]

The traditional concept of liberation (*mukti*) is closely allied to *karma*. The realm of rebirth and *karma* is known as *samsara* and mukti is nothing but liberation from it. This makes our liberation a flight from the world, from the course of history. Our being in this world is thought of as bondage, suffering and alienation. It is 'Liberation *from* the world, not *of* the world.'[8] Kappen brings out the class implications of this false concept of liberation. It leads to the formation of an elite class, the Brahmanas, living 'far removed from the real sufferings of the people.' Pursuing the higher knowledge (*jnana-marga*), they claim superiority over the rest of the society. *Jnana* is the knowledge of the oneness of *Atman* and *Brahman*. To the knower (*jnani*) all his/ her 'inhuman practices are but the play (*leela*) of *Brahman*.'[9]

This concept of human liberation prevented the emergence of collective liberation movements in India.

The doctrine of *advaita* is another aspect of Brahmanism. The non-duality of all indirectly justifies all the crimes. Kappen asks:

> "For, what is wrong with rape, murder, exploitation and oppression if the rapist and the raped, the murderer and the murdered, the exploiter and the exploited, the oppressor and the oppressed are in the end an *Atman-Brahman*?"[10]

It hides all the inhuman social stratification into castes and *varnas*, justified by the doctrine of *varnasrama-dharma*. In *Bhagavad Gita*, Krishna claims to have created the Varna system that keeps in bondage everyone to one's own caste duties. Gita says, "It is far better to perform one's natural prescribed duty, though tinged with faults, than to perform another's prescribed duty, though perfectly. In fact, it is preferable to die in the discharge of one's duty, than to follow the path of another, which is fraught with danger."(BG 3.35)

Rigidity of the Caste System

Kappen traces the root of the rigidity of caste system to the traditional Indian culture that gives primacy to the human body. Human body derives its unique qualities from its birth and is ranked according to its ritual purity or impurity. The pure attain primacy over the less pure or the impure. Thus came into being a hierarchy, the rule of the sacred. One's body derives its status from the family one is born to. So the birth turns out to be the determining factor of ritual ranking. Since one cannot change one's body, or one's parents, ritual ranking is immutable. Born impure, one always remains impure. This made the caste system unchangeable.

The upper castes made use of religious and social sanctions for effecting psychic violence on the rest of the society. Sacred scriptures of the Brahmanas contain numerous tales that prove their claim of racial superiority. Kappen cites an example from *Padma Purana*, of a Brahmana sage Bhrigu stamping his feet on Vishnu's chest. Vishnu reacts, "I am fortunate today, O! Brahmana sage; I am fulfilled in every way, for the touch of your foot upon my body will be a blessing."[11]

In the hierarchical structure of the caste system, everyone feared all those who were above him or her, and was feared by those who were below them. This all-pervasive fear petrified everyone. Morality was determined by this hierarchical caste system. What one ought to do was dictated by the caste to which one belonged, in accordance with the concept of ritual purity. For example, the work of a carpenter was supposed to be prescribed once for all by their Creator (*Viswakarman*). Every human discourse had to be produced in a particular form. A predetermined form was imposed on every human endeavour. This sort of formalism delimited human freedom, creativity, and spontaneity.

Caste System Today

Kappen observes that the members of the upper castes continue to enjoy disproportionate economic power and social prestige. The elected representatives of the people patronize members of their own family, caste, community, or language. This reinforces the sway of tradition within bourgeois institutions. No different is the judiciary.

> "The hierarchy of purity and the hierarchy of merit tend to coalesce without ever fully coinciding."[12]

Buddhism and Hinduism

With the Buddha, the principle of *karma* becomes a theory of freedom. What one does, his karma, has inevitable repercussions on society and nature. Also, one is affected by the *karma* of others. A human, therefore, is a sum of social and cosmic relations. Each person is responsible for the whole of humankind, and the whole of nature. In Buddhism the term *karma-vipaka* refers to the 'ripening' or 'fruition' of the *karmic* potential. For the Buddha, not *jnana* but employing the right means, summed up in the famous Eightfold Path, is the way to liberation.

In the Buddha, Kappen sees a forerunner of Jesus and Marx. Long before the 'Kingdom of God' of the former, and the 'Classless Society' of the latter, we see Gautama preaching a collective destiny for mankind, which he calls 'the Kingdom of Righteousness'.[13]

Buddhism, the protest movement, was gradually absorbed or subdued by the dominant Brahmanic religion. This process continued unabated up to the medieval period. Meanwhile important changes were taking place, in the relations of production. The Brahmanic domination extended to the economic life of village communities, in many parts of India. The Brahmanas got control of the agricultural lands, and the peasants were subjected to exorbitant land-rent taxation. Caste discrimination became more virulent than ever before.

It was as a protest against this, in a religious form that the Bhakti movement emerged. It marked a 'historic mutation in popular religiosity.'[14] Originated in Tamil Nadu, it spread to Maharashtra and Bengal. The movement brought about a new vision of the Divine, and of human's relation to it. The Divine was conceived as the Divine Lover, a personal Deity. Unconditional *bhakti* (devotion) became the principal mode of worship. 'Before the Divine Lover, there is no distinction of sex, wealth, caste or colour.'[15] If God has any partiality it is for those persons destitute of wealth, for the Sudras and the outcastes. The poorer classes formed the bulk of the followers of the Movement.

As in the case of Buddhism, Brahmanism succeeded in subduing or integrating Bhakti movement within itself. Deities, like Krishna and Siva of popular religions, were adapted into the Vedic pantheon through a process of identification or subordination. The Mother Goddesses who originated in the pre-Aryan matriarchal society, were subjugated to male deities. The result was the emergence of Hinduism, as it is known today.

Religious Legitimization of Political Power

Mikhail Bakunin says,

> "It (the State) worships God only because he is its own exclusive God, the sanction of its power and of that which it calls its right, that is to exist at any cost and always to expand at the cost of other States."[16]

This is true of the ruling classes in all societies at all times. They have always found God and religion as means of legitimizing the political subjugation of the masses and serving their class interests.

Kappen cites an example not from Indian history but from the history of the Christian West. In the fourth century, Christianity was proclaimed the official religion of the Roman Empire. Kappen qualifies this event as the "fateful alliance between the cross and the sword, between the imperial Christ and the Christian emperor, an alliance which polluted the mainstream of Christianity down to our days. Later, imperialism of the word and imperialism of the sword undertook the joint venture of colonial conquest."[17]

Secularization

The social phenomenon, called secularization, asserts the society as relatively free from religion. This is the greatest threat to traditional religions. It makes our thinking more rational and emancipates the worldly spheres of life from the control of organized religion. Kappen qualifies that as the coming-of-age of humanity, and welcomes it as 'an instance of the self-liberation of humans in history.'[18] Kappen writes,

> "Emancipated from the sanction of a personal God or an impersonal law (*dharma*), poverty today is viewed as a contingent evil which man is called upon to eradicate through rational means. Thus secularization has created conditions favourable to social revolution."[19]

Conclusion

Originally, as an expression of human transcendence, religion, 'ought to stand for one's freedom from everything that imprisons one within narrow walls.'[20] But in the course of time, religion itself builds walls separating people, and imprisoning many. This in general is achieved by dividing people on the basis of the distinction between the sacred and the profane, the pure and the impure. This division provides legitimacy to the priesthood, ordained to keep the division intact.

Parallel to the social division into the pure and the impure, there arose a division at the individual level as the body and the soul - the soul imprisoned in the body. Religious beliefs emphasized 'the pursuit and realization of the spiritual in humans.' In this perspective, liberation (*mukti*) means the liberation of the soul from the body. Since the body is a part of the material world, spiritual liberation means 'flight from the world of time and space, from the course of history.'

> "Naturally where such attitudes prevail, there is an inevitable devaluation of all temporal activities, whether economic, social, political, or cultural."[21]

Obviously, this sort of spiritualistic conception of religion 'cannot inspire commitment to the creation of a better social order within the pale of history.'[22]

Religious cult probably originated in an attempt to re-enact the primordial cosmic origins, when chaos gave birth to cosmos, the formless to form, and death to life. Whenever the community felt threatened by the forces of death, it chose one among them to die for all, so that from his death would burst forth new life in terms of health, prosperity, children, cattle, and vegetation. Later, a product of labour was substituted for man. In this sense, all sacrifice may be said to have arisen from human sacrifice and has to do with cosmic purification and renewal. Hence all religions, dominated by the notion of purity and rites of purification, are unethical and not really religious.

Religions must return to their primal source, which is the Divine encountered in this our world, *idam sarvam*. Each religious tradition must enrich itself by incorporating elements from the other traditions. This reciprocal acculturation might become true of individual religious experience as well. Kappen says,

> "I, for one, am wary of being called a Christian. I see myself as a disciple of Jesus, who has been profoundly influenced by the teachings of the Buddha and, in theology at least, by the *Siva-Sakti* conception of the divine, going back to the pre-*aryan* culture."[23]

Notes

1. Vol.1, p.118.
2. Vol.1, p.85.
3. Vol.2, p.89.
4. Vol.2, p.93.
5. Vol.2, p.95.
6. BG 2.11.
7. Vol.6, p.15.
8. Vol.5, p.153.
9. Vol.3, p.33.
10. Vol.3, p.33.
11. Vol.5, p.18.
12. Vol.6, p.29.
13. Vol.3, p.219.
14. Vol.5, p.10.
15. Vol.5, p.11.
16. Bakunin 1953.
17. Vol.5, p.30.
18. Vol.1, p.114.
19. Vol.1, p.187
20. Vol.1, p.85.
21. Vol.1, p.27.
22. Vol.1, p.249.
23. Vol.5, p.76.

8

Prophetic Life of Jesus

The Gospel stories about the early life of Jesus tell us what his followers thought of him. Mary is the mother of Jesus and Elizabeth, that of John the Baptist. When both were pregnant, Mary visited Elizabeth. There Mary made a fantastic declaration, part of which is,

> "He (the Lord) has scattered the proud in the imagination of their hearts, he *has put down the mighty from their thrones*, and exalted those of low degree; he has filled the hungry with good things, and the rich he has sent empty away." (Lk 1:51-53).

To Kappen, these words are something tradition puts in the mouth of Mary, and shows Jesus as the subversive presence of the Divine in history. Kappen says,

> "Jesus is here presented as one sent to overthrow the existing relations of wealth and power, to be the herald of a social and political revolution."[1]

The same expectation can be seen in the words of Simeon on seeing the child Jesus.

> "Behold, this child is set for the fall and rising of many in Israel, and for a sign that is spoken against ..." (Lk 2: 34).

In the Old Testament, we can see a long array of people called prophets. They are the ones who revolted against whatever was dehumanizing and committed themselves to the construction of a better future for their society. There are such people in all human societies in all times. This is because, as Kappen says,

> "Prophecy is an essential dimension of individual and collective life in all stages of history."[2]

Prophets emerge in periods of cultural crisis in a society. They give articulate expression to the revolt of the masses against the oppressive social structures and their longing for a future devoid of oppression. So, prophets are heralds of the future, who dream new dreams and see new visions.

> "Their destiny is to leap into the unknown ahead and carry the masses with them."[3]

Both in their revolt against the status quo and their commitment to the not-yet, there is much that is valid for humans of all times. Yet in their vision and achievements, they are conditioned by the status quo they revolt against. They can formulate the future they envisage, only in the language of their time. Though they stand out alone in their vision and commitment, they remain humans of their age.

The mission of prophets is to contradict (negate) the prevalent state of affairs, and hence it is their destiny to be spoken against. They will be contradicted by the guardians of the *status quo*.

> "In this struggle of opposites, the seats of power will fall to the ground and those who were till then made to grovel and slave, will rise up to new humanity."[4]

All prophets are 'invaded by the Divine' and the divinity is radiated through their life. In this sense we can understand the divinity of Jesus too. Thus, the revelation of the Divine in history is continued and it is not a monopoly of any religion.[5]

The Jewish Religion regarded God as revealing himself in historical events. Originally the focus of their faith was the past in which God liberated them from slavery in Egypt and led them to the Promised Land. In the course of time, with the emergence of prophecy, the emphasis shifted from the past to the future. The unjust social structures kindled in them a hope for the definitive intervention of God and a new kingdom of God. This made them critical of social evils. To them the future had meaning only as the final overcoming of the evils of the present.

To Kappen, Jesus was one of the great Jewish prophets like Hosea, Micah, Isaiah, and Jeremiah. He shows this with quotations from the Bible. "A prophet will always be held in honour except in his hometown, and among his kinsmen and family" (Mark 6:4). The same was the reaction of the crowd when he entered Jerusalem, "This is the prophet Jesus, from Nazareth in Galilee" (Matt. 21:11). The Gospels are the response of the early Christians to the life, words, and deeds of Jesus of their time, and hence have to be re-interpreted in our historical context.

While John the Baptist was preaching the baptism of repentance in the river Jordan, Jesus went there. He dipped himself in the river and came up. Then, he saw the heavens torn open and the spirit, like a dove, descending upon him, and heard, "Thou art my son, my beloved; on thee my favour rests."(Mark 1:11)

This is how Jesus inaugurated his public life, as recollected by his disciples. Kappen dwells on the symbolic significance of this narrative, in which the Spirit stands for the power of God. He writes,

> "These symbols, however, do not adequately represent the working of the Spirit. They derive from a patriarchal view of the world where the father is supreme as the source of power, order, and discipline."[6]

Jesus was not wholly free from the male bias of the Jewish society. Still, his self-awareness burst the bounds of male domination.

The Jewish tradition began with the negation of the slavery under the Pharaoh of Egypt. This negation affirmed the hope of freedom in a land 'flowing with milk and honey.' The same dialectic of negation and affirmation, of protest and hope, later found powerful expression in the prophets. Jesus was born into that tradition of historic negation.

> "Jesus stands out as the one great prophet in whose word, deed, and death the dialectic of negativity worked itself out to the full. His *no* to injustice, religious bondage, and political domination at once sums up and radicalizes all previous prophetic protest and project. And the Cross becomes the most telling symbol of man's refusal to be enslaved and his resolve to march forward to fuller life."[7]

In the Jewish society, any breaking of religious laws and cultic practices was considered a sin. Jesus' radical criticism of law and cult was aimed at the liberation of the masses from the bondage of sin. He proclaimed the primacy of mercy over cult.

The kingdom of God proclaimed by Jesus is open to all who have faith in God, revealed by loving one's neighbour. This liberates us from sectarianism and religious bigotry.

> "It makes us free for encountering God in all men of goodwill irrespective of their caste, community or even religion."[8]

Kappen continues,

> "It poses also a challenge for us to pull down all barriers, we
> have created between man and man in the name of religion."

Jesus devalued cult by subordinating it to justice, mercy, and love. He did not project himself as an object of worship. He shifted the axis of religion from the realm of cult and law to that depth-dimension of personal-social life.

Revolt against Religious and Political Powers

Once in his early days, Jesus went into the synagogue. He took the book of the prophet Esaias, and started reading, "The spirit of the Lord is upon me, because he has anointed me to preach the good news to the poor. He has sent me to proclaim *release to the captives and recovering of sight to the blind, and to set at liberty those who are oppressed,* and to proclaim the acceptable year of the Lord" (Lk 4: 18-19). From this Kappen draws the conclusion that Jesus saw the political liberation of his people as an integral part of his mission.

Herod, the king of Judea under the Roman domination, beheaded John the Baptist who criticized him for marrying his brother's wife. Jesus too preached the inviolability of marriage, inviting the wrath of the king. He was once told that Herod was out to kill him (Lk 13:31). Thus Jesus was a threat to Herod.

Jesus was a threat also to the political power of the Sanhedrin, the council of rabbis. His criticism of their cult and traditions was in essence an attack on the religious foundation of their authority. By challenging the authority of the priesthood, siding with the Roman rule, he was in fact undermining the stability of the Roman rule in Palestine. The result was his death on the cross.

In those days, there was a powerful movement of the Zealots fighting against Roman Empire for the restoration of the theocracy of the Sanhedrin. Many found in Jesus a messiah in the line of the Zealots. But he repudiated Zealotism for he aimed not at the restoration of the past but at building a new future.

> "Besides, he did what no Zealot would ever have dreamt of doing: he foretold the destruction of the temple, the very centre, and hearth of the Jewish religion."[9]

Still, towards the end of his life, there was an occasion when Jesus toyed with the idea of armed resistance. As Kappen points out, this is when Jesus tells his disciples to sell their mantles and buy swords. (Lk 22: 35, 36)

The Last Supper

One of the most striking events in the life of Jesus is the Last Supper. Also, celebrated today as Holy Mass, it has been the most controversial issue in the history of Christianity. Let us see how Kappen reads the Last Supper story. Once while he was hospitalized, a few friends visited him. As it was his birthday, they requested him to celebrate it with Holy Mass. As directed by him they brought black coffee and some snacks from a restaurant. Kappen told them about the significance of the Last Supper of Jesus, and shared the snacks and coffee with them.

Being an Asian and a Hebrew, Jesus' way of thinking was concrete, and holistic. To him the words 'body' and 'blood' meant not separate substances but his whole being. He was sharing it with his disciples through the collective gesture of eating and drinking with them. Also the table fellowship foreshadowed the coming kingdom of God. Kappen writes,

> "To interpret the Eucharist along these lines is to bring it down from the rarefied realm of vacuous symbols to the historical

context where it truly belongs: Jesus' table-fellowship with publicans and sinners. It is the western penchant for reducing reality to abstractions that is responsible for the current manner of celebrating the Eucharist where there is no real eating and drinking, not even real bread and real drink, let alone any real commitment to, and anticipation of, the Kingdom to come."[10]

Death on the Cross

The life and activities of Jesus was not only constructive but also subversive as in the conflict with the religious and secular authorities. It came to an end with his death on the cross.[11] Christianity interprets it as a sacrificial offering of his life to God, for the sins of the world. If so, it was a ritual suicide, says Kappen. Jesus did not die a natural death nor did he commit suicide.

> "He was murdered for the sole crime of protesting injustice and domination."[12]

Kappen makes an interesting comment that it is demons that helped the Church make Jesus a God. He proves this, quoting the Gospels where demons, for the first time, call Jesus 'the Holy One of God', and 'the Son of the Most High God.' (Mk 2: 25; 5: 7). For this reason, Kappen calls the demons 'the first theologians.'[13] He adds that Jesus opposed any attempt to make him God. He told the demons, the pioneer theologians, to shut up (Mk 2: 25), and to Peter he shouted, "Away with you, Satan" (Mk 8: 33).

Jesus introduced a new religiosity that seeks to encounter the Divine in the domain of love for one's fellowmen. He demolished the wall between the sacred and the profane by making all humans children of God.

> "The flesh of our flesh, the blood of our blood, he learned to love by being loved by others, gained knowledge of himself in

being acknowledged by others. It was in meeting his kind that he learned kindness and compassion. He loved humans. He struck root in others to such an extent that they became a need for him, especially in moments of crisis. Exquisitely attuned to everything human, he valued the friendship of women; loved children, wine, and the lilies of the field. He could rejoice with those who rejoiced and weep with those who wept."[14]

The death of a prophet makes him/her a mythical figure in the symbolic order of his people. The time he lived in this world is mythicized as lived in the primordial mythical time. Jesus of Nazareth was made into the 'Word that was in the beginning', and Christ the Messiah of the Christian Religion. He was assimilated to mythical beings, and the concrete example of his life ceased to be of any relevance.

Notes

1. Vol.1, p.314.
2. Vol.1, p.33.
3. Vol.1, p.291.
4. Vol.1, p.314.
5. Vol.4, p.208.
6. Vol.4, p.125.
7. Vol.3, p.57-58.
8. Vol.1, p.277.
9. Vol.1, p.80.
10. Vol.1, p.329-330.
11. Vol.4, p.193.
12. Vol.1, p.330.
13. Vol.3, p.179.
14. Vol.1, p.7.

Critique of Christianity

Eclipse of the Historical Jesus

As we have seen in the previous chapter, Jesus the prophet from Nazareth was made into Christ the Messiah and his prophetic movement degenerated into Christianity.

The disciples of Jesus shared the hope of realization of the Kingdom in the immediate future. But, even after the death of their leader their hope was not fulfilled. The social order was not overthrown and the non-privileged remained the same. This had a shattering effect on the very existence of them as a united community. Their leaders were bound to give satisfactory explanations for this failure. Kappen quotes from the second letter of Peter: "First of all you must understand this that scoffers will come in the last days with scoffing, following their own passions, and saying, 'Where is the promise of his coming?' For ever since the fathers fell asleep, all things have continued as they were from the beginning of creation." (2 Pt. 3: 34)

They overcame this predicament by reinterpreting their faith. One interpretation was in terms of divine time as distinct from human time. Peter consoles them saying that 'with the Lord one day is as a thousand years' (2 Pt 3: 8). A more dominant reinterpretation made Jesus the Christ, identified with God. The community still entertained the hope that the Christ would come again to establish the Kingdom. Later, the Church was identified with the reign of God, and salvation was made available only to those having faith in the risen Christ present within the Church. Thus began the proselytizing mission aimed at expanding the Church all over the world.

> "No wonder, the withering away of prophecy and the emergence of mission saw the eclipse of the historical Jesus."[1]

Emperor Constantine declared Christianity as the state religion and accorded economic and political privileges to the Christian leaders.

> "By the Middle Ages, Christianity became a cult-centred religion. Mercy, justice, and love became secondary to the Eucharistic cult and the devotions."[2]

Thus, a prophetic movement against the evils of an organized religion turned into another religion, not much different from the former. The current notion of the Church is that of a community of worshippers of a Christ who remains indifferent to social sins like exploitation, and at the same time over concerned about individual sins like the sexual.

Kappen says,

> "With the downgrading of eros, there came into being within the churches a political economy of guilt, based on the convertibility of the sense of guilt into money."[3]

The movement set in motion by Jesus was predominantly of the poorer classes. Kappen calls it 'primitive Christian communism'. Its motto was 'From each according to one's ability; to each according to one's need'. The Christian leaders, who traffic in the blood of Jesus, wrote it off as utopianism. Kappen says,

> "They forget that they represent the same forces that killed Jesus as well as primitive Christian communism."[4]

Kappen defines social sins as sins embodied in social structure, customs, and laws, and says,

> "A Church that does not fight against these 'demons', is nothing less than an institutionalized betrayal of Jesus."[5]

The kingdom of God cannot coexist with the evils of the world. This contradiction is resolved by the Church by maintaining the dualism of the sacred and the profane, and the spiritual and the material. Its spiritual technicians are ready to purify the profane, the evils of the world.

> "Just as physicians cannot survive without the sick, lawyers without criminals, and social workers without the destitute, so also the Sacred Office in the Church cannot survive without a profane, Godless world."[6]

Dogmatism and the Decline of Prophecy

Dogmatism is the attempt to imprison the Divine in dogmas. For the dogmatist, God is something one can possess as a private property. Such a person cannot have any dialogue with the Divine.

In the earlier pre-scientific age, the universe appeared to humans as having a fixed order. An eternal and immutable cosmos gave birth to similar formulations of faith. But today we find ourselves as living in a world that is changing radically and rapidly - a world that is marching forward. So, the age of dogma is over.

> "We are living in the post-dogmatic age. Henceforth, terms like 'eternal' and 'immutable' have meaning only as qualifying the ultimate horizon, which beckons us from beyond the beyond."[7]

This decline of prophecy was challenged by dissenting movements, branded as heresy by the official Church right from the beginning. Two such movements, started in the second century are Montanism and Marcionism both seeking to defend prophetic authority against institutional authority of the Church.

> "While the official Church relegated women to an inferior position, both Montanus and Marcion tried to assert their equality with men."[8]

Montanus was always accompanied by two women associates, Priscilla and Maximilla, with equal status with him. Understandably all such attempts to revitalize the prophetic movement of Jesus were suppressed by the Church in collaboration with the political powers.

The Second Vatican Council is claimed to have brought out radical changes in the Church. But Kappen is critical of certain declarations of the council. For example, take the statements, 'The Church is the sacrament of salvation for the world.', 'It is her mission to purify and redeem cultures.', 'She speaks in the name of truth itself.' and so on. Kappen says,

> "Such monopolistic claims devalue other religions and constitute a permanent offence to their followers."[9]

Christianity in India

In India's development, Christianity has played a reactionary role. The Christian Churches have built up an institutional empire in the field of education, and health care, thereby bringing under control many secular sectors of socio-political life. This is disavowed by Kappen as it is against the growing spirit of secularism and democracy.

Also, the Churches aim at making 'improvements within the system without transforming it radically.' Keeping in mind the revolutionary prophetic message of Jesus, Kappen writes,

"Hence the historic task of Christianity today is to find a formula of commitment which, on the one hand, meets the objective demands of revolution, and on the other, respects the legitimate autonomy of secular man."[10]

Let us conclude this last chapter with another quotation from Kappen,

"The Christian involved in transformative action is, therefore, better attuned than the worshipping Christian to perceive the truth that Jesus did not die but was murdered by those intent on maintaining the *status quo* in Palestine. It was a perverse theology that converted that murder into death, and the death into a ritual, and the ritual into a mere stepping stone to a resurrection, itself ritualized. It begot a Christianity, which for all practical purposes eliminated the cross and the crucified, a Christianity suited to the affluent West that has 'risen and ascended' to the heavens of conspicuous consumption."[11]

Notes

1. Vol.3, p.26.
2. Vol.4, p.132.
3. Vol.6, p.144.
4. Vol.4, p.148.
5. Vol.1, p.282.
6. Vol.4, p.88.
7. Vol.1, p.260.
8. Vol.3, p.29.
9. Vol.4, p.207.
10. Vol.1, p.255.
11. Vol.4, p.43.

Bibliography

Abbreviations

EW	:	Early Writings
The Origin	:	The Origin of the Work of Art
VE	:	The Vedic Experience

Bachofen, J. J. (1967), *Myth, Religion, and Mother Right,* Routledge & Kegan Paul.

Bakunin, Mikhail (1953), *The Immorality of the State,* The Free Press, NY.

Hegel, G. W. F.(1991), *Elements of the Philosophy of Right,* Tr. H. B. Nisbet, Cambridge University Press.

Heidegger, Martin, *The Origin of the Work of Art* (The Origin), Kappen's translation from German.

Madhusoodanan, G., ed.(2022), *Ecocriticism in Malayalam,* Cambridge Scholars Publishing.

Marx, Karl (1977), *Capital, Vol.1,* Progress Publishers, Moscow.

______ (1975), *Early Writings* (EW), Penguin Books.

______ (1963), *Early Writings,* Trans. T. B. Bottomore, London.

Panikkar, Raimundo (1989), *The Vedic Experience: Mantramanjari* (VE), All India Books, Pondicherry, India.

Sebastian Kappen, *Collected Works of Sebastian Kappen,* ed. Sebasatian Vattamattam, Six Volumes, ISPCK, Delhi.

______ tr., *Kalasrushtiyude Uravidam,* (Malayalam), D. C. Books, Kottayam.

______ *Viswasathil Ninnu Viplavathilekku,* (Malayalam), Edition 3, Pusthaka Prasadhaka Sangham, Kozhikode

______ *A Sexual Morality for Tomorrow,* (Malayalam), Edition 3, Pusthaka Prasadhaka Sangham, Kozhikode

Vattamattam, Sebastian, ed.(2011), *Mariamma Chedathiyude Manikkam Pennu* (Folksongs), N. B. S, Kottayam

Zizek, Slavoj (1989), *The Sublime Object of Ideology*, London; New York: Verso

______ (2009), *First as Tragedy, Then as Farce*, New York: Verso.

Zizek and Milbank, *The Monstrosity of Christ: Paradox or Dialectic?*, (*Monstrosity*) Cambridge and London: The MIT Press.

Collected Works of Sebastian Kappen

Contents of the Six Volumes

Volume I

Part 1: Jesus and Freedom

Preface of the First Edition

Part 2: Essays

Volume II

Part 1: Marxian Atheism

Preface of the First Edition

Part 2: Essays

Volume III

Part 1: Jesus and Cultural Revolution

Foreword

Part 2: Essays

Volume IV

Part 1: Liberation Theology and Marxism

Part 2: Essays

Part 3: Editorial Extracts from Negations

Volume VI

Part 1: Tradition Modernity Counterculture

Preface